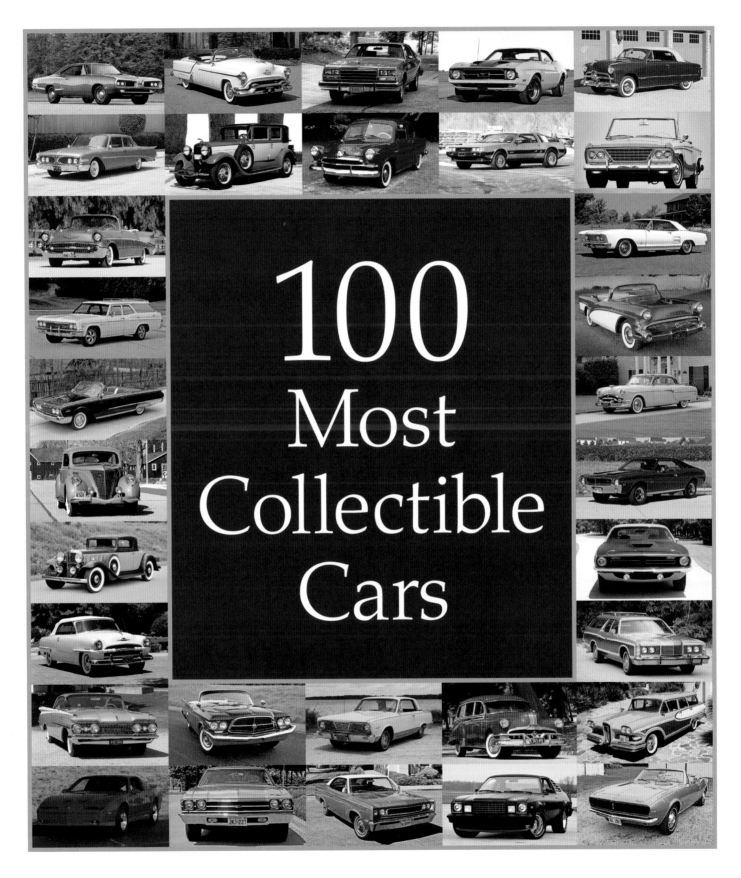

100 Most Collectible Cars

Publications International, Ltd.

Photo Credits

Contents

48

90

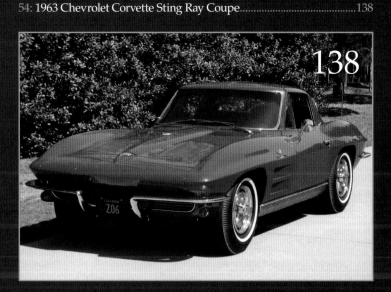

Introduction

If they didn't already know it, anyone who picks up this book will soon surely realize that Americans love to collect cars. Every national club meet, every high-volume auction, and every local summertime cruise night make that abundantly clear.

One possible reason that car collecting has become such a widely indulged pastime (or perhaps obsession to some) is that, as an automotive nation, we've been at it for so long. The automobile started out as an extreme rarity generally priced beyond the reach of the vast majority of Americans. It was looked upon with suspicion, even scorn in some corners. And yet before those conditions had

barely given way to a motorized society in the early twentieth century, people were starting to collect cars.

Consider these few random examples: In 1899, wealthy and well-traveled Larz and Isabel Anderson purchased their first automobile, a brand-new Winton. Nearly every year after, they bought a new American or European car—32 in total—and stored them in the carriage house of their Brookline, Massachusetts, estate as the vehicles became obsolete. As early as 1927, the Andersons started holding weekly showings of their collection.

In Pennsylvania in 1920, successful life-insurance agent W. Emmett Swigart began gathering up "old" cars and

allowed the curious public to drop by his offices to see them. Both the Anderson and Swigart collections became the bases for publicly accessible museums. There were enough like-minded enthusiasts around by 1935 to establish the Antique Automobile Club of America.

The taste for holding onto the objects of automotive history continued to grow, and now almost nothing is out of bounds. Grand coachbuilt classics from the interwar years, baby boomers' muscle cars—even mass-market station wagons brimming with personal nostalgia—are all fair game. Then too, as time goes by, newer waves of collectors expand the definition of "old car." It isn't just running boards or tailfins that identify a car worthy of preservation anymore.

It's this idea that comes through the pages of *100 Most Collectible Cars*. In the 60-year span depicted, there are cars of all kinds of body styles, purposes, and price brackets. A few are one-offs or of extremely limited production. One is a literal museum piece. Others will be warmly familiar to any person who lived in the same time as the car. No body of old-car fans will unanimously agree on what autos are or should be collectible, but this selection of candidates drawn from the vast archives of award-winning *Collectible Automobile®* magazine casts a wide net over the expansive field of what collectors value.

1930
Lincoln Model L
Judkins Berline

A fast car for the Twenties, the Model L Lincoln—with its big V-8 engine—was popular with both gangsters and policemen. It also served to greatly broaden the horizons of the Ford Motor Company at a time when the firm was famous the world over for its simple, hardy, and inexpensive Ford Model T.

The first phase of Lincoln history came to an end in 1930, the last year for the Model L. The Model K of 1931 had a new longer and lower chassis, but retained an improved version of the faithful Lincoln V-8. A V-12 would follow a year later, establishing itself as the signature Lincoln engine into the late Forties.

Henry Leland, who had been the father of Cadillac, also founded Lincoln. He insisted on the highest standards of engineering and construction. Unfortunately, he didn't put much effort into the appearance of the new marque. Dull styling and a recession led to receivership. Henry Ford bought Lincoln in 1922; Leland left in a huff just a few months later; and Ford's son, Edsel, assumed management of the new acquisition.

Edsel was good for Lincoln. Leland had created an outstanding chassis, but the junior Ford had the taste needed to make the car look good. No detail was too small to be considered. For instance, in 1925, Gorham silversmiths designed a chrome greyhound mascot for the radiator cap—an item that would grace Lincolns until the last Model K was delivered in January 1940. (It was molded using the "lost wax" process, a method that consistently gave fine detail. No less than Rolls-Royce also used the technique to fashion its iconic "Spirit of Ecstasy" mascot.)

Edsel Ford enhanced Lincoln's image by ordering custom bodies from the leading coachbuilders in lots of 10 to more than 100. This provided distinctive coachwork at a more reasonable price than one-of-a-kind custom bodies. Among the firms contracted for this work was John B. Judkins of Merrimac, Massachusetts. Its specialties for the Lincoln Model L were a two-passenger coupe and variations of the berline four-door sedan.

Judkins built four versions of the berline, a term derived from the German city of Berlin. This 172-A with two side windows and a retractable divider between the front and rear seats was one of 42 built in 1930. It features a distinctively angled windshield invented by Brewster coachbuilders. The configuration was thought to reduce glare and improve visibility in rain. It found some popularity in the

Twenties but had almost disappeared by 1930. While a "standard" factory-bodied Lincoln sedan cost $4500, Judkins berline prices started at $5600.

As introduced for 1921, the L-head V-8 with cylinder banks angled at 60 degrees displaced 357.8 cubic inches and made 81 bhp—though Ford claimed 90 horsepower from '22 on, even after boosting displacement to 384.8 cubic inches in 1928. The powerplant employed costly fork-and-blade connecting rods that allowed a rod from one bank to straddle a rod from the other bank on the same crankshaft journal. Power went to the rear axle via a three-speed transmission and torque-tube driveline.

Early on, there had been two wheelbase lengths, 130 and 136 inches, but soon only the longer span was used

(save for a 150-inch "commercial" chassis). Beginning in 1927, all Lincolns came equipped with four-wheel mechanical brakes, a feature first seen a few years earlier on Prohibition-era police-pursuit specials. Other chassis features found on the 1930 Lincolns were a worm-and-sector steering gear (with a new, faster ratio), double-acting Houdaille hydraulic shock absorbers, and 20-inch-diameter wire-spoke wheels. A shock damper was added to the left front wheel to reduce shimmy.

The Lincoln Model L is an enduring testament to its maker's attention to engineering, craftsmanship, and beauty. Indeed, the Classic Car Club of America recognizes the entire series as one of its "full classic" automobiles.

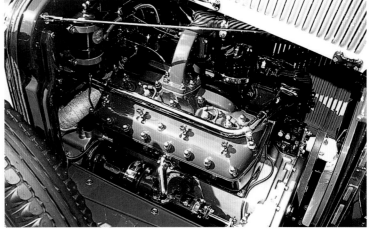

1932
Nash Advanced Eight Coupe

Experience is reputed to be a good teacher. Even before Charles Nash cut his teeth in the automobile business running Buick in the Teens, he had worked in the carriage business for General Motors founder William Durant. Wild spending had cost Durant control of GM once, and when he was poised to regain control of his creation in 1915, Nash knew his careful, frugal nature would not mesh with the "new" boss. He left to start his own car company, Nash Motors.

The company steadily prospered through the Twenties, helped by Charlie Nash's attention to costs and prudent control of production. The well-regarded 1929 series-400

cars became even grander for 1930 with the addition of an inline eight-cylinder engine with overhead valves as well as Nash's "Twin Ignition" system of dual ignition coils and two spark plugs per cylinder. This helped produce more complete combustion for improved fuel economy and eliminated cylinder ping and knock.

For '31, there were three eights in the fold, an L-head powerplant with conventional ignition and two Twin Ignition jobs. This trio (and the base L-head six) carried over into the run of "first-series" 1932 cars, only to be replaced by larger-bore eights when the "second-series" Nashes were announced in March.

The largest of these engines was a 322-cid job that generated 125 bhp and was undergirded by nine main bearings for strength and smoothness. This mill went into the Advanced Eight series, a five-car line set on a 133-inch wheelbase; and the new Ambassador Eight, composed of four long sedans (including a limousine) astride a 142-inch span between the wheel centers.

All second-series cars were graced with "Slipstream" styling that featured lower lines, a semibeavertail rear, slanted windshield sans visor, a vee'd radiator, tapered parking-light housings atop the front fenders, and vent doors in place of louvers in the hood sides. Cars powered by either of the ohv eights also featured lowered ride heights as a result of receiving a new worm-drive rear axle—for which Nash boasted 500,000 miles of reliable operation. Period fad Free Wheeling—ostensibly a fuel-saver—was a new option.

The Advanced Eight coupe shown here had a starting price of $1695; only the four-door sedan undercut it at a savings of $100. It was only available with a rumble seat for maximum four-passenger capacity. Anyone seeking a two-seat business coupe had to shop in the Big Six, Standard Eight, or Special Eight lines.

Charlie Nash's careful ways proved sound in Depression-wracked 1932. Even though reported retail sales fell by almost 50 percent from the year before, Nash Motors still earned a profit of slightly more than $1 million—this after paying out in excess of $4 million in dividends to company stockholders.

The array of elegantly styled and impressively long Nashes ran through 1934. Their fine quality hasn't gone unnoticed. The Classic Car Club of America accepts higher-line models like the Advanced Eight for membership.

The harsh effects of the Great Depression on luxury-car sales forced Packard to reconsider its attachment to grand, meticulously built cars that sold for more than $2500 and ranged up to near $8000. In 1935 Packard would enter the upper-medium-price field with a series built on mass-production principles in search of greater sales volume. It was a move that would ultimately change the nature of the company and its products.

Before that could happen, however, the revered marque pressed on through the early Thirties as it always had, with cars of impeccable quality and impressive appearance. Indeed, for 1932 it joined the brigade of so-called multicylinder cars with a V-12-powered line as the new flagship.

Still, the majority of Packards were motivated by L-head inline eights. There were two in the early Thirties, one of 319.2 cubic inches and another of 384.8 cid.

The 1933 Super Eight series was outfitted with the larger engine. Annual increases in power had pushed it to 145 bhp by '33. That year the Packard engines shifted to downdraft carburetion—a Stromberg two-barrel—and gained an automatic choke and dual coils.

A new double-drop frame with a strengthened "X" member in the middle that came in for '32 was continued, but with slight shifts in wheelbase. All but one of the 14 Super Eight models were on a 142-inch stretch. A feature dubbed "Ride Control" provided driver-selected damping and a new power-operated braking system presented four pedal-pressure settings to call the 14-inch-diameter drums to service.

Styling for the '33s evolved with skirting on the trailing edges of fenders, a deeper vee'd radiator, and a little more rake to windshields. Headlamps now appeared to be freestanding without a tie bar between them (though a hidden rod through the grille enhanced rigidity).

Closed cars like the $3090 jump-seat-equipped Super Eight seven-passenger sedan incorporated "Packard Ventilation Control" with front-door windows in two sections that pivoted at opposing angles. Typical of the industry's interest in trying to improve cabin ventilation at the time, it unfortunately worked better in theory than in practice and wasn't continued for 1934.

1934
Pierce-Arrow
840A Coupe

In the early years of the American auto industry, the "Three Ps"—Packard, Peerless, and Pierce-Arrow—were the top luxury cars. Perhaps the most exalted was Pierce-Arrow, said to be so exclusive that the Pierce board of directors and clientele were one and the same. Pierce-Arrows were in the White House garage from the Taft Administration into the FDR years.

But there was more to the Pierce reputation than snobbery. The carefully engineered cars were built

with the finest materials and craftsmanship, which resulted in solid reliability. The Glidden Tour tested the reliability and endurance of early cars, and Pierce won the event from 1905 through 1909. Pierce-Arrow came out of the World War I years with an enviable reputation and customer loyalty.

Then Pierce faltered in the Twenties with outdated design and engineering. The company was on the ropes by 1928, but it had a design for a modern car with a new

straight-eight engine. Studebaker bought the company and supplied the capital to introduce this completely new Pierce-Arrow. The new car was a runaway success with almost 10,000 sold for 1929—a company record. Momentum kept Pierce profitable for the first year of the Depression. A V-12 engine debuted for 1932. By 1933, however, Studebaker was in receivership and Pierce-Arrow sales had fallen to 2152.

A group of businessmen from Buffalo, New York, Pierce-Arrow's home, bought the company from Studebaker for $1 million. This newly independent Pierce-Arrow brought out a restyled car for 1934 with both eight- and 12-cylinder

engines, but sales remained elusive—registrations for the year came to just 1740 cars. Pierce managed a redesigned car for 1936, but the company failed in 1938.

The '34s were introduced in three revised and renumbered series, the eight-cylinder 840A and the V-12 1240A and 1248A. (Come April, a revived 836A added a lower-priced eight to the mix.) Appearances were freshened with a painted grille shell, a quartet of horizontal hood vents per side, and dipped-center bumpers. Closed-body cars added draft-free vent wings.

The 840s were powered by a 385-cid L-head inline eight, effectively the return of an engine last used in 1931 but with a six-percent output increase to 140 bhp at 3400 rpm. Among its features were hydraulic valve lifters. Pierce was one of the first to use them in pursuit of quiet operation.

About half of the available series-840A body styles—the $2895 coupe with rumble seat among them—rode a 139-inch wheelbase; the rest, including a new Silver Arrow fastback coupe that traded on the name of a 1933 show car, used a 144-inch spread. An interesting Pierce engineering feature was a foot-shaped brake pedal connected to mechanical brakes with transmission-driven power assist—a system known to be tricky to modulate at low speeds.

1935
Hupmobile
W-517 Coupe

Hupmobile had a long and sometimes contentious history. Founder Robert Hupp spelled his name with a double "p" but the name of his car contained only one, unless abbreviated to Hupp. When the first Hupmobile, the Model 20, bowed in 1909, it was priced even lower than the new Ford Model T.

The founder soon left the company, and Hupmobile moved up to the medium-price field, where it established a strong reputation for quality and dependability. Hupps were solely four-cylinder cars until 1925, when they were joined by a straight eight. When a six was added for '26, the four was dropped.

Hupmobile was moving further upmarket and even offered custom bodies for the eight. In 1928 it had attractive new styling by Amos Northup, who later designed the influential and acclaimed Reo Royale and Graham "Blue Streak." Sales reached a record of 65,862 cars. Nineteen twenty-nine should have been even better, but sales started slipping even before the stock-market crash.

Like other makes, Hupp's sales declined precipitously in the Great Depression. Advanced styling by famed industrial designer Raymond Loewy (later known for his Studebaker work) failed to stop the slide. Battles in the boardroom and courts should have finished off Hupp, but it struggled on.

The least-expensive Hupp model of 1935 was the W-517 coupe at $695—the lowest ever for a Hupmobile. Murray

supplied bodies to both Hupp and Ford, and the W-517 shared some sheetmetal with the '34 Ford to cut costs. Northup, called on again for its design (initiated as the 1934 W-417), added a unique grille, hood, and fenders for distinction.

Presented in four body styles and a choice of base or DeLuxe trim, the W-517 was something of an outlier among Hupmobiles due to its "conventional" styling. All other '35s had the streamlined "Aerodynamic" look—with headlamps faired into the hood sides—penned by Loewy. When an Aerodynamic-bodied D-518 six was added in January, the W-517 was soon discontinued after a production run of 2586 units.

The W-517's 224-cid L-head six was boosted to 91 bhp. The series rode on a 117-inch wheelbase with Hupp's unusual "Chassis Torsional Stabilizer," a triangular system of tubular underhood braces that was said to create a more rigid front structure.

Hupp sold 10,781 cars for the 1935 model year, and its fortunes fell rapidly after that. The factory shut down due to lack of funds for '36 and much of '37. New models arrived for 1938, just in time for a sharp economic downturn. A plan to use Cord body dies for a Hupp Skylark didn't really get off the ground, and production ceased in July 1940. The company wasn't quite dead, though. It reorganized in time to get defense contracts in World War II.

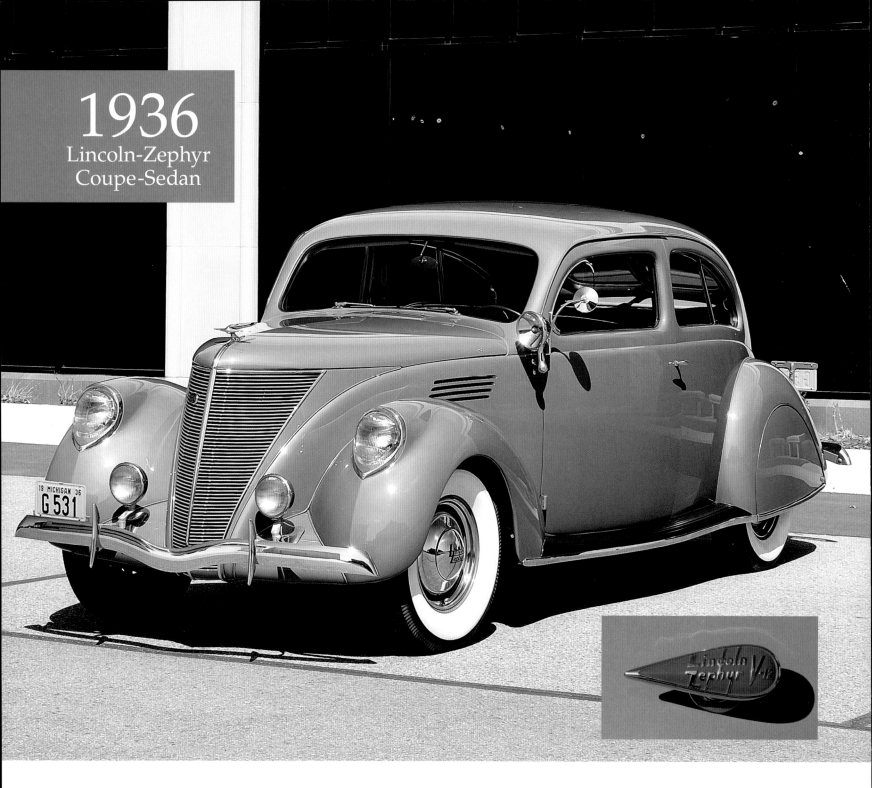

Advanced streamlining came to American automobiles in 1934 with the Chrysler Airflow, but it didn't truly begin to gain acceptance until the arrival of the Lincoln-Zephyr two years later. The Zephyr managed to look futuristic without seeming alien—unlike the water-fall-front Airflow.

The roots of the Lincoln-Zephyr design were laid down by John Tjaarda, an immigrant from the Netherlands who had imagined a whole series of cars that were not only sleekly styled, but also full of advanced construction ideas.

However, his ideas didn't begin to approach fruition until he was hired by body supplier Briggs Manufacturing, which wanted to present some advanced designs to the Ford Motor Company, one of its clients.

Front- and rear-engine mock-ups of the teardroplike con-cept were paraded before the public at various exhibi-tions—an early form of market research. Roughly half of respondents favored a front-engine layout, but almost nobody liked the car's radically sloped nose. When Ford chose to put the car into production for 1936, it insisted on a more upright front. The prowlike vee'd grille and pointed alligator hood were soon imitated throughout the industry, which validated the correctness of its design.

The Zephyr served as a lower-priced companion car to the carriage-trade Model K Lincolns, and began narrowing the gaping price chasm between Fords and Lincolns. Still, it wasn't cheap. Initial body styles were a $1320 four-door sedan and a two-door "Sedan-Coupe" that started at $1275. (A $1425 Town Limousine sedan came later.) That put the Zephyr up against the likes of the Cadillac-companion LaSalle and Packard's lower-cost One Twenty.

Those competitors were eight-cylinder cars, but the Zephyr packed a V-12. The 267-cid L-head engine was created specifically for the new car, albeit with many standard Ford V-8 parts to manage development costs. It made 110 bhp.

The Zephyr was constructed from an early type of unitized construction. Being a Ford Motor product, however, its chassis utilized some extremely traditional elements like transverse leaf springs for suspension and mechanical brakes.

From 14,994 made for '36 (including 1814 Sedan-Coupes), the Zephyr would rise to be Lincoln's savior in the Forties with the demise of the august Model Ks.

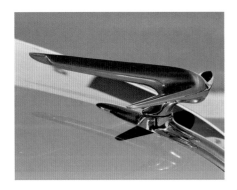
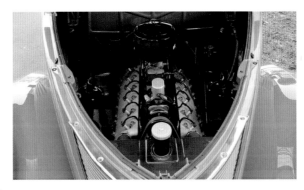

1940
Mercury Eight
Convertible Coupe

In 1938, a gap of about $600 existed between the price of the Ford DeLuxe Fordor sedan and the company's Lincoln-Zephyr sedan. That was enough to buy a base Ford coupe. Ford Motor Company was missing out on sales in the $800–$1400 market.

Edsel Ford had long wanted a medium-price car to fill the hole between Ford and Lincoln. While General Motors buyers could start with a Chevrolet and move up the Pontiac-Oldsmobile-Buick-LaSalle-Cadillac ladder, Ford customers had no place to go unless they became affluent enough to buy a Lincoln. That got a little easier with the introduction of the upper-medium-price Zephyr in 1936, but there was still a big void. Henry Ford—who called the shots—finally gave his son the go-ahead to create such a car for the 1939 model year.

Edsel might have admired the GM "car for every purse and purpose" policy, but he didn't slavishly follow that

formula. While GM tried to give each make a separate style and identity, Edsel planned a super-deluxe version of the Ford DeLuxe. The new car clearly shared a styling theme and engineering with its Ford sibling. In fact, Edsel wanted the new car badged "Ford-Mercury." Chief stylist E. T. "Bob" Gregorie convinced Edsel at the last minute that the car should have a separate identity. Still, some early cars had "Ford-Mercury" on their hubcaps before "Mercury" hubcaps could be made.

Mercury's 116-inch wheelbase was four inches longer than Ford's, and sedan bodies were nearly eight inches wider. Mercurys were about 130 to 200 pounds heavier than similar Fords. Although styling was in the same vein, Ford and Mercury didn't share any body panels. The differences extended into the interiors—Mercury was better trimmed and equipped.

Ford had developed a larger 239.4-cid version of its 221-cid V-8 for truck and police-car duty, and that engine

was pressed into service for Mercury. The 95-bhp Merc engine had 10 more horses than the 221. This gave the Mercury sedan a better power-to-weight ratio of 32.7 pounds per horsepower, versus 34.1 pounds for Ford. Ford had sprightly performance, but the Merc was hotter still with a top speed of more than 90 mph. Mercury also got better gas mileage thanks to a higher gear ratio. The successful new make ranked 10th in sales for its first year.

For 1940, badges were changed to read "Mercury Eight." The gearshift lever moved from the floor to the steering column and styling tweaks showed up on the grille, taillights, and bumpers. A shift to sealed-beam headlights was accompanied by new chrome bezels. The convertible coupe gained a vacuum-powered top of either black or tan fabric. Starting at $1079, the ragtop attracted 9741 customers.

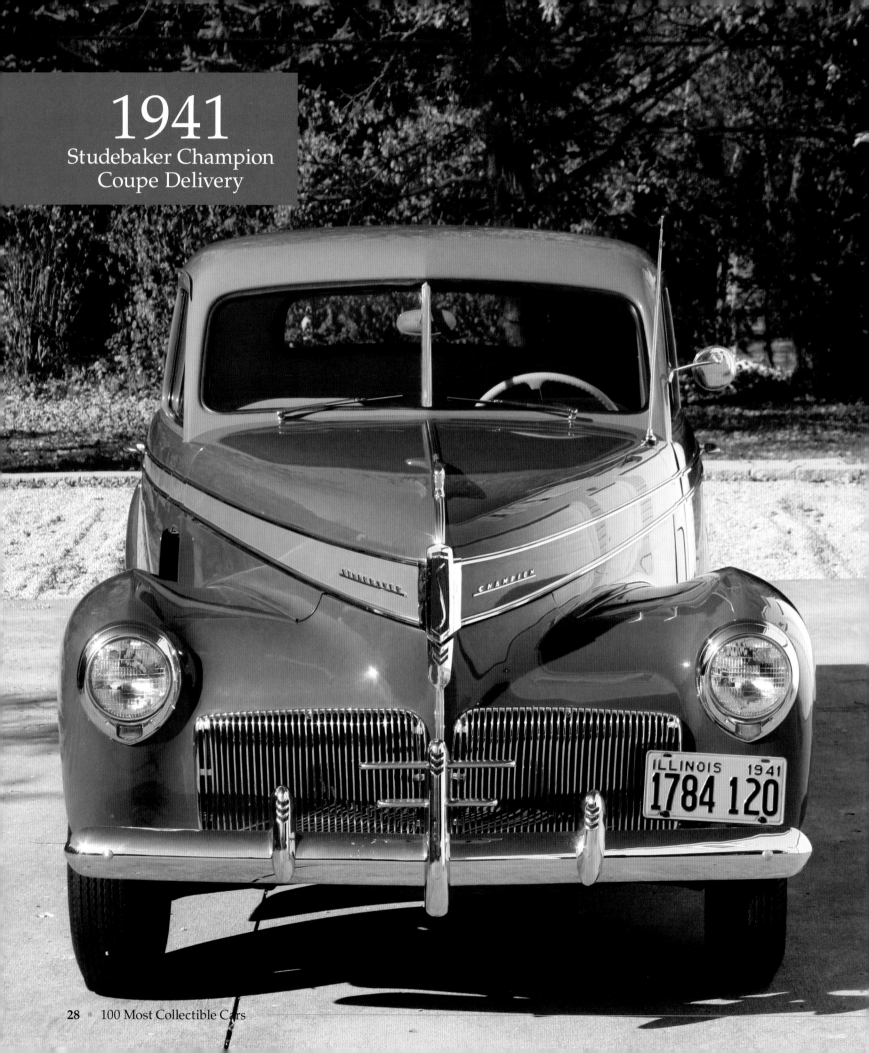

1941
Studebaker Champion
Coupe Delivery

ILLINOIS 1941
1784 120

Transformable vehicles have come and gone over the years. General Motors once sold the Chevrolet Avalanche and Cadillac Escalade EXT—both were an SUV and a pickup. The GMC Envoy XUV had a retractable rear-roof panel that converted the SUV into a sort of pickup à la the 1963–66 Studebaker Wagonaire with its retractable roof section that allowed the station wagon to haul tall items. But those weren't the first such efforts.

From late 1939 through 1941, Studebaker sold the Champion Coupe Delivery. It blended a three-passenger business coupe with a pickup bed that could be inserted into the trunk cavity to take up the slack at a time when Studebaker lacked a regular light-duty pickup.

The coupe/pickup idea had been around since at least the mid Thirties with Chevrolet, Ford, Plymouth, and Terraplane all offering versions. Competitive automakers are always looking for a new niche, and the coupe/pickup was a vehicle that could make light deliveries when needed and then convert back to a car. Today, we think nothing of using a pickup for a night on the town, but in the prewar Champion's day people were about as comfortable arriving at a restaurant in a truck as they were wearing shorts to the office. Although a clever idea, coupe/pickups never sold in large volume.

Studebaker's Coupe Delivery bed was made by Edwards Iron Works. The firm, located about a mile from the main

factory in South Bend, Indiana, had a long association with Studebaker, supplying truck beds and other components. The Coupe Delivery bed was 68 inches long, 30 inches wide, and 18.63 inches deep. It was light enough that one man could lift it. Studebaker claimed it could be installed by two men in 45 minutes. The trunklid could be replaced when the bed was not in place. The bed cost $31 in black or $33 if color matched to the body. A canvas cover cost $9, and there was an available header to separate the cabin from the bed.

The Coupe Delivery was based on the least-expensive body style of the entry-level Champion family, which was redesigned for '41 with new bodies that housed wider seats and incorporated more glass area. The well-thought-out and engineered Champion had given Studebaker a foothold in the low-price field in '39. Rather than confront the "low-price three" directly, Champion was a little smaller and significantly lighter. This allowed it to offer

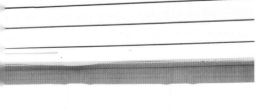

competitive performance with better fuel economy. Champion was a success and helped to put Studebaker on its firmest financial footing since the boom times of the Twenties.

Champions rode on a 110-inch-wheelbase chassis that used Stude's "Planar" transverse-leaf-spring independent suspension up front. They were powered by an L-head six that had been designed expressly for the new product line. Launched at 164.3 cid and 78 bhp, the powerplant was enlarged to 169.6 cid and 80 bhp for 1941.

The '41 Champion Coupe Delivery shown depicts the premium Delux-Tone version with standard two-tone paint. The base price of a Delux-Tone coupe was $780, and in addition to the color-matched bed, this one sports options that include overdrive ($45), Climatizer heater/defroster ($35), fender skirts ($12.50), radio ($47.50), and clock ($10.50).

1942
Buick Special Station Wagon

The beautiful Buick Special Estate Wagon was General Motors's most luxurious wagon for 1942. Cadillac was content to leave such cars to other GM divisions and never offered a production station wagon in the U.S. until the CTS Sport Wagon of 2010–14. That left Buick the top dog of GM's wagon offerings from 1940 until the last Buick Century and Roadmaster station wagons of 1996— and then a brief revival in 2018–20 with the all-wheel-drive Regal TourX.

Buick built a few wood-body depot hacks in 1923 (set on a short-lived truck chassis), but it wasn't until 1940 that the division cataloged its first real station wagon based on the new midrange Super chassis. For 1941, the wagon moved to Buick's less expensive Special range. That doesn't mean that the Estate Wagon became any less big or stylish. It rode the generous 121-inch wheelbase of Specials that used GM's "B" body (a subseries of shorter A-body-based Specials was added that year). Like other Buicks, it featured all-coil-spring suspension and torque-tube drive, and the Special shared their styling.

Appearances were updated for '42 with front fenders that flowed into the doors and a distinctive wide grille with vertical teeth, a look that was destined to be a Buick trademark for many years. Specials could be outfitted with extra-cost

rear fender skirts that were standard elsewhere in the line.

They also shared an ohv straight-eight engine. Century, Roadmaster, and Limited models had a 320.2-cid engine, while Special and Super used a smaller 248-cube version. For 1941, the Special engines developed 115 bhp with a single carburetor or 125 bhp with newly available "Compound Carburetion" that utilized two sequential two-barrel carbs. In '42 those figures fell to 110 and 118, respectively, as cast-iron pistons were substituted for aluminum to free up the latter material for growing defense-production needs. The car on these pages is equipped with Compound Carburetion.

The Special was vitally important to the division. When Harlow Curtice took over as general manager of a staggering Buick in November 1933, he made development of a lower-priced line a priority. Launched as the Series 40 in spring 1934 (it wouldn't get the Special name until '36), it

soon became Buick's best seller in the prewar years.

The Estate Wagon's wood body was built by the Hercules Body Company of Evansville, Indiana. Hercules also supplied wagon bodies for the other General Motors divisions, as well as for Packard. Hercules used high-quality ash framing with mahogany panels.

Tailgate-mounted taillights were hinged so that they could function with the tailgate lowered. Oddly, a right-side brake light was optional. Buick was the first to have standard turn signals, in 1939, and the rear turn signals were incorporated in the emblem below the tailgate. The turn-signal lever was mounted on the right side of the steering column, under the shifter.

The wagon weighed 3925 pounds and cost $1450, making it the heaviest and costliest member of the '42 Special lineup. Only 328 Estate Wagons (out of 46,715 total Specials) were produced for the war-shortened model year.

1942
Chrysler Town & Country Station Wagon

By the late Thirties the utilitarian station wagon was developing a cachet similar to today's luxury SUVs. However, upscale Chrysler didn't have one until 1941. To make up for the late start, Chrysler Division General Manager David Wallace planned a luxury wagon designed to be more streamlined and stylish than competing models.

While other wagons mounted a wooden box behind sleek front sheetmetal, Chrysler streamlined the entire vehicle. The rear was a semifastback or "barrelback" design. It was the first wagon with a steel top, a stamping shared with Chrysler's limousine. The new creation was badged Town & Country—a nameplate subsequently used almost continuously by Chrysler through 2016.

Chryslers of the period had bulletproof construction and the Town & Country was no exception. The ash frame and mahogany panels were milled by a Chrysler subsidiary. A section of Chrysler's Jefferson Avenue plant in Detroit was devoted to the laborious task of assembling the wood-and-steel body practically by hand.

Town & Country was available as a six-seater or as a nine-passenger version with three rows of seats. The middle seat folded similar to limo jump seats. The rear bench could either pivot back to provide legroom with the jump seat folded down, or forward to create more cargo space. Leather upholstery was standard.

Alone among American station wagons of the day, the T&C featured a side-hinged "clamshell" tailgate that opened at the center. The fixed metal roof might have complicated the process of loading tall items, but the people doing the loading could get right up to the cargo floor without a drop-down tailgate in the way.

The Town & Country was mounted on Chrysler's 121.5-inch-wheelbase six-cylinder chassis. The 1941 Town & Country was part of the base Royal line, but moved up to the better-trimmed Windsor family for 1942. The L-head six, bored out to 250.6 cid for '42, developed 120 bhp. Chrysler's Fluid Drive torque converter that eliminated some clutch use and Vacamatic semiautomatic transmission were standard.

The generation of Chryslers extant in 1942 dated to 1940. Annual styling updates gradually expanded the reach of the grille's horizontal bars to the point where they now wrapped fully around the front of the car.

T&Cs accounted for about 2000 sales between 1941 and '42 before World War II ended production. The timbered Town & Country returned in the postwar years, but in convertible, sedan, and hardtop-coupe versions. The name finally returned to wagons in mid 1950.

1942
Dodge DeLuxe Business Coupe

Dependability had been the watchword at Dodge since Horace and John Dodge built their first car in 1914. With war clouds gathering as the 1942 line was introduced in late 1941, dependability became even more important. Many car buyers had a sinking feeling that the '42 model they were buying might have to serve through the duration of a coming conflict.

To introduce its 1942 cars, Dodge made a promotional film with Jimmie Lynch of *Jimmie Lynch's Death Dodgers*, an auto-daredevil show that—perhaps appropriately—used Dodges. Lynch drove the new Dodge over railroad ties, sent it airborne off ramps, and finished with his "roll of death." The Dodge was battered, but still drivable. This was more than hype. Dodges of that era weren't excitement machines, but they were solid and dependable.

Among the improvements for '42 was a bigger L-head six-cylinder engine. Enlarged from 218 to 230 cid, its horsepower rating rose from 87 to 105. Fuel economy became a concern with the imposition of wartime gas rationing, but Dodge held up its end. In spite of its bigger engine, Dodge was able to boast that, in a nationwide test, its '42 model averaged 21.64 mpg.

Optional Fluid Drive came to Dodge in 1941 and was still heavily promoted in '42. Fluid Drive replaced the flywheel

with a fluid coupling. Slippage in the coupling allowed the car to come to a complete stop while in gear without releasing the clutch. Fluid Drive also reduced the need to downshift from high in the three-speed gearbox. One could even start from a dead stop in high, although acceleration off the line was leisurely. Lynch demonstrated hill climbing with Fluid Drive by stopping halfway up a flight of concrete stairs, then resumed climbing by only pressing the accelerator. For drivers of the day, accustomed to fancy footwork with a clutch and accelerator to start up steep grades, this must have seemed like a miracle. No other car in Dodge's price range offered Fluid Drive's convenience of reduced shifting and clutching.

A full complement of glistening chrome indicates a car built before mid-December '41. At that point, government "blackout" rules required that bright trim be eliminated or painted over. It wouldn't be long before all auto production itself would be halted to make way for defense work.

Nineteen forty-two Dodges underwent an extensive facelift with a lot of new sheetmetal. Of the 68,522 built for the abbreviated model year, 5257 were DeLuxe-series three-passenger business coupes, a body style not found within the costlier Custom series. The proportions of the close-coupled roof and long rear deck imparted something of a chopped-top look. The business coupe was the least expensive '42 Dodge at $895 to start.

1946
Ford DeLuxe
Tudor Sedan

Fords of the Thirties and Forties were famous for their V-8 engines, a feature that left them virtually without peer in the low-price field. From its 1932 introduction, Dearborn's side-valve "flathead" was a sensation, and—ultimately—an inspiration to a new generation of hot rodders. But for much of the Forties, there was a second engine that lived in the shadow of the V-8.

Henry Ford was no fan of six-cylinder engines, an aversion that dated back to his unpopular Model K of 1906–08. Still, he could not ignore the clamor from within his dealer body to satisfy customers who perceived the V-8 to be less economical than competitors' sixes. With a push from son Edsel, the company patriarch agreed to an inline six that bowed for 1941.

It was an L-head design like the V-8, but, at 226 cid, it actually had more displacement than the vaunted Ford eight. Indeed, it was the largest-displacement six in its market segment. It generated 90 bhp, which led to the V-8 being rerated at 95 horsepower, and it even developed more torque.

When civilian auto production resumed after World War II with 1946 models, the Ford six picked up where it left off in '42—save for a switch to a Holley one-barrel carburetor. More extensive modifications put in place late in the '47 model year raised output to 95 bhp, where the engine stayed until being replaced for 1952 by a totally new six with overhead valves.

The six-cylinder-powered 1946 Ford Tudor sedan shown (a two-door sedan so named as a mate to the four-door Fordor model) is an excellent example of what the average American bought when auto production resumed after World War II. Many had a long wait before their new car was delivered. There were more buyers than new cars in 1946, even though automakers resorted to meeting pent-up demand with prewar designs that pretty much relied on trim and detail changes to seem new.

Body shells and dimensions basically dated to 1941, with plenty of tried-and-true Ford engineering underneath everything. Set on a wheelbase of 114 inches, the chassis sported Ford's cherished transverse-leaf-spring suspension front and rear, plus torque-tube drive.

Nineteen forty-six Fords came in base DeLuxe (shown) and top-line Super DeLuxe trim. DeLuxes had an ashtray, armrest, and sun visor on the driver's side only. Super DeLuxe buyers got two of each. A clock was an option for DeLuxes; a painted plate took its place to the right of the radio on cars without it. The Super DeLuxe also had a more colorful interior, but the exteriors were nearly identical.

Many dealers gave preference to customers who ordered accessories such as front fog lights, a heater, and a radio. The Ford radio had an unusual face with three dials. The left dial was for "tone-scale" adjustment. The narrow center dial showed numerical presets selected by the touch bars or an "M" for manual tuning. On the right was the conventional radio dial. A foot control could select presets or, with a light press, mute the radio.

The DeLuxe Tudor started at $1136 as a six-cylinder car, $49 less than its V-8 sidekick (now with a 100-bhp 239.4-cid mill under the hood). A combined six/V-8 production total of 74,954 made it Ford's third most-popular car in '46. The company built 468,022 of its model-year 1946 cars, which made it number one in a year in which manufacturers fitfully resumed operations amid material shortages and strikes.

1947
Chevrolet Fleetmaster
Fleetline Aerosedan

et's say you're not convinced that appearance is an
important factor—maybe *the* important factor—that
drives car shoppers to choose one vehicle over another. Then consider the 1947 Chevrolet Fleetline Aerosedan.
Despite being the most expensive two-door closed car in
the Chevy lineup, it was still the most popular model of the
best-selling brand in America in '47.

Why? After all, mechanically, it was the same as any of
Chevrolet's other 10 models offered that year. In standard
equipment, it varied little from most cars in the Fleetmaster
series out of which the two-car Fleetline subseries was
derived. It had to be the looks.

Aerosedans had the benefit of fastback styling that was very much in vogue in the Forties. General Motors gave the style a big boost in 1941 when it launched a well-received armada of B-body Pontiac, Oldsmobile, Buick, and Cadillac sedans and coupes. When a fastback roofline was extended to the A-body program in 1942, Chevrolet jumped on the bandwagon with the Aerosedan.

An instant hit, this two-door companion to the notchback Sportmaster four-door sedan (another trendy style introduced in 1941 as the first Fleetline model) topped the Chevy sales charts in '42. When production resumed for 1946, the Aerosedan slipped back into the pack, but then shot back up into sales leadership the next two years. The 159,407 Aeros built in 1947 tallied 23.7 percent of all division passenger-car production. Another 211,861 were made for '48 before the aging prewar design was replaced.

Aside from its distinctive roof, the Aerosedan came with a trio of chrome spears on each fender and special "Fleetweave" upholstery fabric that were Fleetline series exclusives. Otherwise, from its 90-bhp ohv 216-cid six to its 4.11:1 rear axle, the Aerosedan was a lot like most Fleetmaster models. And that was a good thing. When evaluating the 1947 cars for *Mechanix Illustrated* readers, influential car tester Tom McCahill opined that the Chevy "will undoubtedly remain one of America's top cars from the standpoint of popularity. . . . The dependability of the Chevrolet is beyond question."

1948
Tucker '48
Four-Door Sedan

During World War II, a number of entrepreneurial types in the U.S. foresaw a postwar world of consumers clamoring for new cars after being denied the chance to buy them while the nation's auto plants had been turned into arsenals. Trusting that the established automakers couldn't meet all the demand right away, these dreamers saw a chance to get into the business.

Preston Tucker was one of the most ambitious of this group. He got his start in the car business as a salesman in the Twenties and was behind Ford's factory-supported— but unsuccessful—bid to win the 1935 Indianapolis 500. Then, in 1944, he began laying plans to build a car of his own, "the first completely new car in fifty years."

Not only would the Tucker '48 (as it formally came to be called) look different than anything on the road, it would be engineered differently, too. Imaginative stylist Alex Tremulis came up with the essential fastback design with prominent rear fenders, aircraft-type doors cut into the roof, a horizontal teardrop effect for the front fenders, and a central headlamp that turned as the front wheels were steered. Independent suspension was employed at all four corners of the 128-inch-wheelbase sedan, and occupant safety was stressed in features like a pop-out windshield, padded

crash cowl, and even a "safety chamber" into which a front-seat passenger was encouraged to drop in the event of an imminent collision.

The rear-mounted engine—a six-cylinder helicopter power-plant with opposed cylinders and converted to water cooling—displaced 335 cubic inches and made 166 bhp. Tom McCahill of *Mechanix Illustrated* was able to go from zero to 60 mph in 10 seconds in a Tucker.

Tucker secured a former bomber plant in Chicago to build the car, which was priced at $2450. However, in late May 1948 the federal Securities and Exchange Commission began an investigation of the company over suspicions about some of its financial dealings. The next year, Tucker and seven associates were tried on federal charges that came out of the probe. They were found not guilty on all counts in January 1950, but the damage was done. Including the "Tin Goose" prototype, the sum total of Tucker production came to just 51 cars.

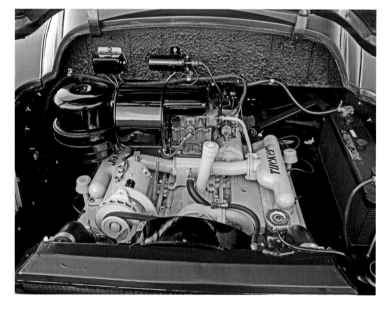

1949
Ford Custom Convertible Coupe

"There's a Ford in Your Future" was the company's advertising slogan after World War II, but the future of Ford was questionable as, by some accounts, the company lost $10 million a month in 1946. Henry Ford's brilliance launched one the world's most important companies, but in his declining years he resisted change and made decisions that left the company in chaos. Son Edsel's death in 1943 left Henry's young grandson, Henry Ford II, the heir apparent. With pressure from his wife Clara, old Henry reluctantly turned over the reins to "HFII" in September 1945.

Henry Ford II had his work cut out for him. Ford had to build a new management team and replace an outdated product line. Ford Motor Company's future was riding on the all-new 1949 Ford.

Fortunately, it was a home run, a result all the more surprising considering the company ditched its original plans for a new postwar car on the fly and hastily sought a different design concept. With its flush sides and straight-through fenders, the new Ford made competing postwar efforts from General Motors and Chrysler Corporation look old-fashioned. Plus, the new Ford was four inches lower than the old model. Not only did the car look good on the outside, but it had more room inside.

Old Henry had clung to the Model T's transverse leaf-spring suspension and torque-tube drive for way too long.

The new Ford had an up-to-date coil-spring and independent front suspension. The rear sported parallel leaf springs and Hotchkiss drive. The engine was shifted forward, which moved the back seat ahead of the rear axle for a smoother ride. "Flathead" six-cylinder and V-8 engines returned with the same 95- and 100-bhp ratings, respectively, but there were new combustion chambers and improvements in the cooling and lubrication systems.

The new Ford was the company's most thoroughly redesigned car since the Model A, and it also had the biggest introduction since the Model A. Some 28 million flocked to dealerships in the first three days. Production for the model year came to 1,118,759 units, which put Ford in front of archrival Chevrolet by almost 94,000 cars—although Ford's extended model year (introduction of the '49s came in June 1948) most certainly provided an advantage.

Still, not everything was rosy. The '49 was rushed into production and there were problems. Although the body looked great, it was poorly engineered and prone to flex, rattles, and leaks. Moving the engine was good for ride, but it caused steering and handling problems. Ford engineers soon busied themselves with making the updated 1950 models "50 Ways New . . . 50 Ways Finer" in response.

The 1949 Fords came in two series, Standard and Custom. Standards offered two- and four-door sedans and two coupes, one of which was a three-passenger business model. The Custom series included both sedans, a club coupe, a two-door "woody" station wagon, and a convertible that cost $1949 (with V-8). With 51,133 units produced, it was the most popular convertible in the country.

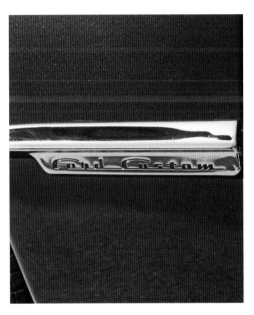

1949
Oldsmobile 88 Deluxe Two-Door Club Sedan

The new kinds of cars produced after World War II—once the early carryovers had run their course—called for a new kind of engine. General Motors was ready to deliver such a powerplant, a short-stroke ohv V-8 with a relatively high compression ratio, for 1949.

Engines of this type appeared first in Cadillacs and senior Oldsmobile 98s. Then, on February 6, 1949, Olds added a second V-8 series, the 88. It featured the division's "Rocket" V-8 in a smaller, lighter package that made the brand synonymous with speed at the start of a horsepower race that would accelerate into the early Seventies.

The Rocket displaced 303.7 cubic inches. Outfitted with hydraulic valve lifters and a two-barrel carburetor, and subject to 7.25:1 compression, it developed 135 bhp at 4500 rpm and a stout 263 pound-feet of torque at a low 1800 rpm. Dropped into an 88 body, it immediately became a tempting tool for racers. In fact, five of the eight events in NASCAR's very first season of races for late-model sedans were won by Olds 88s.

At Olds, the 88 and six-cylinder 76 series used GM's "A" body, which was fully restyled for 1949 along the lines set down for bigger C-body cars in '48. Notchback and fastback body styles were offered, and most came in a choice of standard or Deluxe trim. Springing an extra $131 for Deluxe gear garnered two-tone upholstery, foam-rubber seat cushions, aluminum sill plates, a fancier steering wheel, wheel trim rings, and more.

Oldsmobile produced more than 100,000 first-year 88s in spite of the late introduction. The Deluxe Club Sedan (Olds's nomenclature for the fastback two-door sedan) accounted for 11,820 of them. It cost $2300, a tab that covered the Hydra-Matic four-speed automatic transmission that was standard in all 88s.

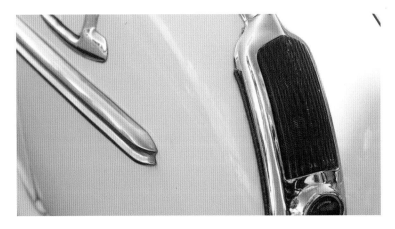

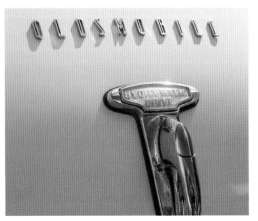

1950

Chevrolet DeLuxe
Styleline Four-Door Sedan

T he styling of the first all-new postwar Chevrolet wasn't as advanced as that of its rival, the '49 Ford with its smooth flanks and fenders that flowed in an unbroken line from front to rear. However, the Chevy did have pleasing lines and a junior-Cadillac look that was well received by the public.

The design was lower than previous models and the engine was moved forward, which benefitted interior room. The two style-setting Fleetline models of recent years were expanded upon for 1949 with two- and four-door fastback sedans called Fleetlines and notchback sedans and coupes labeled Stylelines, all in a choice of two trim levels.

While styling was all new, the chassis was only refined. There was revised front suspension with tubular shock absorbers replacing lever shocks. The venerable Chevy 216.5-cid ohv six (its architecture dated to 1937) was massaged, but maintained a 90-bhp rating.

For 1950, there were only minor detail changes to the Chevrolet's appearance, most notably substituting two "stanchions" beneath the parking lights for the series of grille teeth that were found on the '49s. The big newsmakers were the introductions of the Powerglide two-speed torque-converter automatic transmission and the Bel Air hardtop coupe, both firsts in the low-price field. To compensate for certain driveline inefficiencies, Powerglide cars got a larger 235.5-cid 105-bhp engine with hydraulic lifters, but even standard-transmission jobs with the mechanical-lifter base six saw output increased slightly to 92 horsepower.

The 1950 Chevrolet model seen here, a DeLuxe Styleline four-door sedan, was the marque's most popular choice for the year. Priced at $1529 to start, it drew 316,412 orders. (Its DeLuxe Fleetline counterpart cost the same but saw 192,000 fewer assemblies.) DeLuxes came with more external brightwork and nicer interior features and materials than the fairly austere Special-series cars, all for a $79 premium (in sedans). It was a fee that most customers gladly paid; demand for DeLuxe models swamped the distribution of Specials.

The car pictured has the standard three-speed manual transmission with synchronizers on the top two gears, but no longer with the sometimes-troublesome vacuum-assisted shift mechanism that was dropped after 1948. Extra-cost options on the vehicle include a heater, pushbutton radio, and reverse lights. One thing it doesn't have is electric turn signals, something motorists take for granted today. Chevrolet added them to its accessory list in 1940 but wouldn't standardize blinkers until 1955.

While Ford won the model-year sales derby for 1949 with its lengthy production run, Chevrolet took back the top spot in 1950 by a margin of 139,000 cars. (Both brands turned out well more than 1 million units each in what was a record sales year for the auto industry as a whole.) Chevrolets of the era were competitively priced. Plus, they were well built and reliable, which also served to boost their popularity.

1950
DeSoto Custom Station Wagon

The wood-bodied station wagon was in its twilight years by 1950. It had progressed from commercial depot hack in the Teens and Twenties to something of a status symbol in the Thirties and Forties. Station wagons were just the thing for hunting trips or carrying riding tack to and from the stables. In the 1939 movie *Dark Victory*, Bette Davis's socialite-horsewoman character describes herself as part of the "station wagon crowd."

By then wagons were well styled and crafted. The fine wood suggested yachts—and required almost as much maintenance. Proper care meant annual varnishing—but even then the wood could rot and sections would need to

be replaced. Changes in temperature caused wood to expand or contract. Screws and bolts had to be tightened periodically to avoid squeaks and rattles.

Meanwhile, families of more average means noticed that wagons could be well-suited in carrying a growing family and its gear. However, the station wagon was often the most expensive body style in its manufacturer's lineup, and nobody wanted to add varnishing the family car to the list of regular household chores. The steel-bodied station wagon changed that, and a new kind of station wagon crowd was more likely to be seen at Scout jamborees or PTA meetings than at horse shows.

Willys and Crosley built the first all-steel station wagons right after World War II, but the Crosley was a tiny subcompact and the Willys was a little more trucklike—almost a sport-utility vehicle—with Jeep-inspired styling. The first mainstream full-size steel wagon was the popular 1949 Plymouth Suburban. By 1953, Buick was building the last American wagons with structural-wood components.

DeSoto was a latecomer to the station wagon field, having just offered its first factory-cataloged job in 1949. Like that year's Dodge Coronet and Chrysler Royal wagons, it was a nine-passenger car with decorative ash framing over metal body panels. The '50 incorporated some important changes. It became a six-seater with a handy fold-down second-row seat and, like the Dodge and Chrysler, replaced the two-piece transom tailgate with a window that retracted into the tailgate, a feature destined to be widely copied. Only 600 of the $3093 wood-trimmed wagons were built for 1950, plus another 100 very-late-arriving full-metal haulers. The psuedo-"woody" would not return in 1951.

The upright styling beloved by Chrysler Corporation President K. T. Keller worked well on the DeSoto station wagon. For the 1950 facelift of the '49 design, there was a new variation of the brand's toothy grille, and a new hood ornament that featured the helmeted head of Hernando de Soto with a plastic face that glowed when the headlights were lit. However, while other models got squarer rear fenders with integral taillights, wagons retained the fall-away fenders and separate taillights of the 1949 cars.

Underhood was a 236.6-cid L-head six that produced 112 bhp. The engine was more impressive than its specifications. The six was smooth and a good hill climber. It included a high-compression head, a well-engineered ignition system, and low-friction Superfinish internal parts to reduce wear. A three-speed manual gearbox was standard on base DeLuxe models, while Customs had a semiautomatic transmission dubbed "Tip-Toe Hydraulic Shift with gýrol Fluid Drive" that was, for the time, as close as the brand could get to one of the increasingly popular automatics.

1952
Pontiac Chieftain Station Wagon

The 1952 Pontiacs sported the third in a series of styling updates to the basic design instituted for 1949. A slightly revamped grille, fresh trim, and redesigned wheel covers were the major appearance changes.

The slow-selling Streamliner fastback sedans were discontinued, as were the price-leader business coupes. All remaining models were now marketed as Chieftains and, depending on body style, standard, DeLuxe, and Super DeLuxe trim levels were available.

Chieftain station wagons came in standard trim with three-row seating for eight passengers or as a DeLuxe model that had room for six in two rows of seats. Second- and third-row seats could be removed for greater cargo-hauling flexibility but lacked the convenience of folding seats.

Pontiac wagons continued to use the all-steel body that replaced the traditional "woody" during the '49 model year. However, the body still employed stampings embossed and decorated to resemble the birch and mahogany woodwork that had been used previously.

The most important change for the 1952 Pontiacs may have been to the optional automatic transmission. Dubbed Dual-Range Hydra-Matic, the improved gearbox offered two drive positions and came paired with a new "economy" rear axle that used a 3.08:1 ratio.

The gear selector's left "DR" position used four gears for reduced engine revolutions that promoted fuel economy, quieter operation, and longer engine life. This range was best suited to highway or light-traffic use.

The right "DR" setting used only the first three gears to provide better acceleration and flexibility in heavy traffic. This position also increased engine braking when descending long hills or mountain roads. Selecting "Lo" allowed the car to start in second gear, a great advantage on icy roads.

The new Hydra-Matic was only available with new high-compression (7.7:1) versions of Pontiac's six- and eight-cylinder inline L-head engines. The high-compression head raised the output of the six to 102 bhp from 100 and the eight to 122 bhp from 118. Cars equipped with the three-speed manual transmission came with the base powerplants as standard. The extra oomph was warranted because the Hydra-Matic outweighed the Syncro-Mesh manual by 125 pounds.

Road tests of Pontiac Eights with the Dual-Range Hydra-Matic appeared in the April 1952 issues of *Motor Trend* and *Science and Mechanics*. Both spoke highly of the new transmission, with the former declaring it "undoubtedly the best compromise between the stick shift and the fluid coupling; it has the 'shifting ability' of one, combined with the ease in shifting of the other."

Pontiac promotional literature touted this powerteam "For the performance thrill of your life" and, by far, Pontiac buyers preferred the eight-cylinder engine and the Dual-Range Hydra-Matic transmission. More than 90 percent of the 271,373 customers for the division's '52 models chose the 268.4-cid eight, which cost about $75 more than the six, and more than eight in 10 bought the automatic.

The eight and Dual-Range Hydra-Matic weren't the only choices made for the Chieftain station wagon seen here. The car wears a sunshade, fender skirts, lighted hood ornament, full wheel covers, and extra brightwork including headlight rings and gravel shields that were not included in the vehicle's $2689 base price.

1953
Buick Skylark
Convertible Coupe

With Buick's golden anniversary on the horizon, division general manager Ivan Wiles spotted designer Ned Nickles's drawings for a customized Buick convertible. Wiles liked what he saw, and a show car dubbed Skylark made the rounds in '52 with plans for the rakish ragtop to be a limited-production model for Buick's 50th year in 1953.

Perhaps coincidently, Cadillac Eldorado and Oldsmobile Fiesta convertibles were also on the show circuit in preparation for the 1953 model year. Once in production, none of these three flagship droptops were big sellers, but they added glamour to the lineups and helped pull customers into showrooms.

The Skylark brought European touches to the Buick Roadmaster convertible. Door tops were dipped in parallel to the distinctive, flowing fenderline found on that year's C-body "senior" Buicks, and wheel openings were fully radiused to reveal chromed Kelsey-Hayes wire wheels. The windshield was chopped so the car stood less than five feet tall with the top up. Missing from the front fenders were Buick's signature "ventiports"; smoothed rear-quarter panels did away with a horizontal character line found on Roadmaster and Super models.

The Buick brochure called Skylark an "American sports car"—a stretch since it was a six-passenger, 4315-pound car riding on a 121.5-inch wheelbase. Still, the Skylark looked much sportier than the brand's other convertibles.

The Skylark's chopped version of the standard Roadmaster windshield didn't require a modified cowl like the Eldorado and Fiesta with their panoramic windshields, but there were still enough special body panels to drive up the sticker price. Cost was further increased by a long list of standard equipment that included power-assisted steering, brakes, seat, windows, and top. A signal-seeking radio and leather upholstery were also included. (Indeed, a continental-kit spare tire was the lone option on offer.)

All of that ran the list price of a Skylark up to $5000 when a Roadmaster ragtop cost $3506 and $4144 fetched a Cadillac Series 62 convertible. Perhaps that's why only 1690 of the super-deluxe Buicks were sold.

Buick had a new V-8 engine for its anniversary. Prior to World War II, Buick's top straight eight was one of the most powerful available, but it was falling behind in the postwar horsepower race as other makes brought out better-performing V-8s. Buick's new 322-cid ohv V-8 with up to 188 bhp put the marque back in the race. Also upping performance for '53 was a new version of Buick's Dynaflow automatic transmission that added a second turbine wheel for more torque multiplication which improved acceleration. Twelve-volt electrics were newly employed for V-8 cars.

Despite the limited demand for the 1953 Skylark, it did not vanish as a "one and done." There was a 1954 version, albeit based on the B-body Century. Buicks were all new for '54 and maximum output of the 322 V-8 was raised to 200 horsepower. However, despite this and a $517 price cut, Skylark orders were more than halved to just 836 units. The car may have faded but the name was too good to lose. Starting in 1961, it graced a string of compact and midsized Buicks into the late Nineties.

1953
Henry J Corsair
Two-Door Sedan

Henry J. Kaiser revolutionized shipbuilding during World War II with his mass-produced Liberty ships. While Kaiser was building ships faster than anyone had ever imagined, he was already planning to shock the auto industry with a postwar "people's car." As early as 1942, Kaiser was concocting a front-wheel-drive, fiberglass-bodied car to sell for as little as $400. However, when the Kaiser bowed as a 1947 model, it was a conventional, medium-price sedan.

The realities of getting a car into production forced Kaiser to abandon his unorthodox ideas, but he never gave up on the idea of creating a people's car. When a radical design for a tubular-framed economy car was presented to him by a Detroit industrialist, he jumped at it even though his chief engineer said it was impossible. The engineer was right: Production cars were more conventional with a traditional ladder frame.

Kaiser stylists and consulting designer Howard "Dutch" Darrin didn't like the fast-back body and offered other proposals. Although those proposals were rejected, Darrin was asked to assist the in-house styling team in refining the selected design.

The new 100-inch-wheelbase compact made its debut in 1951 as the Henry J. (Kaiser-Frazer Corporation ran a name-the-car contest, but that was a PR stunt; the company knew from the beginning the car would be named in honor of the boss.) Although regarded as a separate make, the letter "K" appeared in several places on the car as a reminder that it was a Kaiser product.

Willys provided engines, a 68-bhp, 134-cid four and an 80-bhp, 161-cid six, both L-heads. The four was Willys's "Go-Devil" engine that also powered Jeeps. Helped by a curb weight of only 2293 pounds, the Henry J delivered fuel economy in the mid to high twenties. Prices started at a reasonable $1219 for the four and $1343 for the six.

Road testers of the time thought the car was lively with good handling. Tom McCahill,

driving a six, did 0–60 mph in 14.8 seconds and reported a top speed of 84 mph. For comparison, in *Motor Trend* tests, a '51 Ford V-8 automatic went from zero to 60 in 17.82 seconds and topped out at 87.25 mph.

While Henry J performance was quite good for an economy car, there were also complaints that it was too Spartan, lacking a glove box, dome light, and—early on—even an opening trunklid. At first, a folding rear seat provided the only access to the trunk. Initial acceptance was good, with nearly 82,000 sold for the 1951 model year, but then declined rapidly. Nineteen fifty-four would be the last year for Henry J.

A 1952 facelift with a new grille design and taillamps in the tiny tailfins was carried over into 1953, when a four-cylinder Henry J Corsair cost $1399. (A six-cylinder Corsair DeLuxe sold for $1561.) Acknowledging gripes about the car's starkness, a glove box, dome light, and opening trunklid had all become standard along the way. The folding rear seat was retained as an option. The list of extra-cost upgrades included items like a passenger-door armrest, bumper guards, and full "Dinosaur Vinyl" upholstery. Kaiser's head of color and trim, Carleton Spencer, created this die-stamped alligator-grain vinyl that proved extremely tough and long wearing.

Kaiser wasn't alone in probing the market for compact cars in the early Fifties—Nash, Willys, and Hudson built similar vehicles, and a growing trickle of small autos from Europe was making the voyage to America. However, the Henry J showed that buyers craved something more from their small car than just a low price.

1953
Oldsmobile Fiesta
Convertible Coupe

M any people remember Zsa Zsa and Eva Gabor, but few know that there was a third Gabor sister, Magda. Magda didn't appear on screen or talk shows, but she lived an interesting life and is said to have been part of the Hungarian resistance during World War II before escaping Nazi-occupied Europe.

The 1953 Oldsmobile Fiesta just might be the Magda Gabor of cars. General Motors built three bold convertible concept cars for the 1952 show circuit and then put them in limited production for '53: Cadillac Eldorado, Buick Skylark, and the Fiesta. The Eldorado was the most powerful and expensive, while the Skylark had the sportiest styling and the best sales. They received the most attention when new and have been the subject of countless magazine articles since. If the Fiesta is mentioned at all, it's usually as the trio's "Oh, and don't forget . . ." member.

The Fiesta was based on Olds's top-line Ninety-Eight convertible. It rode on a long 124-inch wheelbase and had room for six passengers. Oldsmobile accelerated America's

horsepower race with the ohv "Rocket" V-8 of 1949, and its performance was even more potent for '53. The Rocket displaced 303.7 cubic inches and produced 165 bhp in Super 88s and Ninety-Eights, but, for the Fiesta, a slight compression boost raised output to 170.

Fiesta was further distinguished from the Ninety-Eight convertible by a new wraparound windshield that was also a few inches lower than stock. GM's panoramic windshield would sweep the industry during the Fifties (indeed, all Oldsmobiles would have one for '54), with Fiesta and Eldorado preparing the public for this next styling craze. There was also a slight dip in the beltline over the doors. These subtle differences required modified sheetmetal for front fenders, hood, and doors.

The Fiesta was priced at $5715, or $2516 more than a regular Ninety-Eight soft top—enough extra to buy a Super 88 sedan. Other features unique to the Fiesta included a special leather interior in three available color combinations, distinct chrome trim, spinner wheel covers, and avail-

able two-tone paints. (The last two items would be available on other Oldsmobiles in 1954.) Most Fiestas were two-toned, with the deck and upper rear quarters in a contrasting color, but some painted in solid black or white are known to exist among surviving examples.

The symmetrical dashboard was standard Olds fare with a large, circular instrument cluster balanced by a big radio speaker with a centrally-mounted clock situated in front of the passenger. However, the dash was modified slightly to mate with the new windshield. To help justify the high price, Olds loaded on the equipment. Standard on Fiesta were power steering, brakes, windows, and seat; "Autronic Eye" headlight dimming; signal-seeking "Wonder Bar" radio; heater/defroster; whitewall tires; and "Super Drive" Hydra-Matic automatic transmission.

An attractive convertible with all those features wasn't enough of a draw to overcome the hefty price and only 458 Fiestas were sold. Oldsmobile dropped the Fiesta after 1953, but kept the name around to use for station wagons in later years. Although a sales flop, the Fiesta was a nice halo car that previewed several styling features destined to appear on Oldsmobiles in the next few years.

1953
Packard Mayfair Hardtop Coupe

Packard's neglect of its luxury line took a toll on the fortunes of the respected automaker in the Fifties. It needed medium-priced cars to survive the Depression. It also needed men skilled in the production and selling of volume-built cars. The new executives brought in to create and launch the successful One Twenty eventually held sway in the company and had low regard for the senior Packards that required far more man-hours to produce than the mass-produced cars that bore the name.

The neglect of the luxury line meant that Packard lost ground to Cadillac. Although luxury cars usually lost money in the Depression, Cadillac was back to making money hand over fist by the Fifties. In 1952, Packard gained a new leader in James Nance, a marketing expert from General Electric's Hotpoint appliance division. Nance felt that if Packard were to survive, it needed to get serious about its luxury cars again. To him, that meant dividing the marque's senior and junior product lines.

Nance arrived a year after Packard's 1951 redesign. The bathtublike styling of the 1948–50 models had fallen out of favor, but Packard's latest styling was up to date. The new line was divided into the medium-price 200 series (renamed Clipper in 1953) on a 122-inch wheelbase and the senior 300 and Patrician models on a 127-inch span. Both were powered by Packard's renowned—but aging—L-head straight eights at a time when the ohv V-8 was beginning to dominate the industry.

The hardtop coupe body style was increasingly popular, and Packard's first was the 1951 Mayfair. Although built on the shorter 122-inch wheelbase of the junior line, the Mayfair had the larger 327-cid straight eight and the better trim of the senior series. It was placed in an "in-between" 250 Series that also included a convertible.

Nance wanted to make the Mayfair more of a senior car and ordained plusher trim for 1953. Engineering increased compression ratios, and the Mayfair's 327-cube eight saw horsepower increase from 150 to 180 bhp. This was short of the Cadillac V-8's 210 bhp, but definitely in the Buick range. Packard also added power steering and air conditioning to the options list—further proof that Nance was serious about the luxury market. The '53 Mayfair—which now found itself in an unnumbered "base" series with a

pair of convertibles, including the highly customized Caribbean—cost $3278 and 5150 units were built.

The best fruits of Nance's efforts to reestablish Packard as the top American luxury car came to market in 1955 via a new line with powerful V-8s and advanced torsion-bar suspension. But quality-control issues and Packard's financial crisis, which was heightened by its 1954 merger with Studebaker, killed a noble attempt, and Packard was soon an orphan make.

1953
Plymouth Cranbrook Convertible Coupe

n 1953, the U.S. economy was robust and Americans were spending. Bestowed with fresh stying, Plymouth set a record with almost 650,000 cars built to hold its number-three sales position behind Chevrolet and Ford—as it had since 1931. Nineteen fifty-three was also Plymouth's 25th anniversary, but it chose not to celebrate. Perhaps with Ford and Buick marking golden anniversaries that year, Plymouth felt like an upstart.

The restyled, slab-sided Plymouth was smoother, rounder, and sported the brand's first one-piece curved windshield. A new instrument-panel design moved the glovebox to the center, where it could be reached by driver and passenger alike. All Plymouths now rode on a 114-inch wheelbase, a change from the previous four years when model lines were perched on 111- and 118.5-inch wheelbases. At a time when the competition was getting bigger, Plymouth's overall length actually shrank an inch.

However, Chrysler Corporation management was more concerned with function than form. Interior room—head room in particular—counted for more than a sleek silhouette. Although lower than the previous year's car, the new Plymouth still appeared tall and upright compared to the competition.

Ride was a functional concern, too, and Chrysler Engineering made sure that Plymouth's suspension, with its patented "Oriflow" shock absorbers, was the best of the "low-priced three." The engine was a dependable 217.8-cid L-head six that dated back to 1942. With only 100 bhp, Plymouths were less powerful than Fords or Chevys, but they were also lighter, so performance was comparable. Plymouth was the only make of the three still without an automatic-transmission option, but at midyear a semiautomatic was added. Dubbed Hy-Drive, it replaced the flywheel with a torque converter and eliminated much of the need for shifting and clutching, all for $146.

Plymouths came in two trim levels: base Cambridge and better-equipped Cranbrook. The $2220 convertible was the most expensive model, and was naturally a Cranbrook. The soft top and all other two-door models had a new "E Z Exit" front seat with the seatback divided in a one-third/two-thirds split. This allowed a front passenger to slide to the center of the seat while the outer third was folded forward to allow rear passengers to get in or out. Cranbrook convertibles enticed 6301 customers with their charms.

After the record sales of 1953, Plymouth production for '54 fell to fewer than 463,000 cars, slipping to fifth place behind surprise third-place claimant Buick and fourth-place Oldsmobile. A concerted sales battle between Ford and

General Motors, along with Plymouth's "practical" looks, worked against Chrysler's high-volume brand.

But Plymouth fought back. By 1955, it had fresh Virgil Exner "Forward Look" styling, available V-8 power, and a PowerFlite fully automatic transmission. Sales topped 700,000 that year. Two years later, Plymouth was once again in its accustomed third place.

1954
Ford Customline
Two-Door Sedan

Just judging by outward appearances, the 1954 Fords certainly seemed to be mildly updated continuations of the 1952–53 models. There was, however, much more going on under the surface. Indeed, they were the ones that were the most "different" of the three-year run.

For starters, Ford retired its famous "flathead" V-8 and replaced it with an ohv V-8—a year before chief rival Chevrolet debuted its vaunted "small-block" V-8. (The change applied to U.S.-built Fords; those manufactured in Canada retained the L-head mill through '54.) Curiously, this new V-8 had the same 239.4-cubic-inch displacement as the last flathead. A deep block that retained a crankshaft supported by five main bearings caused it and its descendants to be referred to as "Y-block" engines. The short-stroke engine's kidney-shaped combustion chambers were subject to a 7.2:1 compression ratio, and a two-barrel carburetor meted out fuel. With 130 bhp, it put out 20 more horsepower than its predecessor.

Ford's overhead-valve six was not neglected in this year of advances. Introduced in '52 at 215.3 cid and 101 bhp, it was bored out to 223 cubic inches and saw power climb to 115 bhp.

Also new was a front suspension that followed in Lincoln's footsteps and replaced king pins with ball joints for improved durability. The switch was accommodated by a 0.5-inch stretch in wheelbase, which now stood at 115.5 inches. Brake drums for station wagons grew a full inch in diameter to 11 inches.

Exterior styling alterations were minimal—a new design for the central grille bar and revised parking-light placement, plus a full-length stainless-steel side molding for middle- and top-range models. A greater change took place inside, where a new instrument panel recessed most controls within a strip of tooled aluminum. The speedometer was now a domelike "Astra-dial" with a window of green translucent plastic on top that would illuminate the face with natural light. However, "idiot light" warning lamps replaced true oil-pressure and amp gauges. New convenience options included power windows and a power front seat.

Fords came in three series: base Mainline, midrange Customline, and top-shelf Crestline. It was a growing family, with a two-door Ranch Wagon added to the Customline series and a four-door sedan and Skyliner hardtop augmenting Crestline offerings. The Skyliner featured a tinted Plexiglas section in the roof above the front seat.

The majority of Ford shoppers flocked to the Customline series. Its five models offered them things like dual sun visors, door armrests, a half-circle horn ring, automatic dome light, clock, foam-rubber seat cushions, and more that didn't come standard in Mainlines. Extra-cost items like whitewall tires, exterior mirrors, an AM radio, and power brakes—among other things—were available to make them safer and more comfortable. In fact, the Customline two-door sedan was the best selling 1954 Ford with 293,375 built. The base price of the V-8-powered two-door Customline with standard three-speed manual transmission was $1820.

It was all good for Ford. The division made 1,165,942 cars for the model year—beating Chevy by 22,381 units.

1955
DeSoto Firedome Convertible Coupe

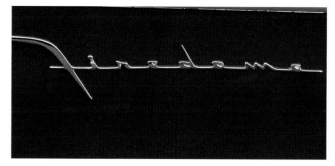

Had Virgil Exner become a designer of buildings rather than cars, he would have been an advocate of Louis Sullivan's belief that "form follows function." Known for his innovative design work for Pontiac and the Raymond Loewy studio, Exner produced vehicles that showcased his approach to automotive design, "art made practical." One notable example of this philosophy is the 1955 "Forward Look" DeSoto.

Named for explorer Hernando de Soto, the cars were supposed to appeal to the owner's sense of adventure. But uninspired, boxy postwar cars became the antithesis of this spirit. With sales of all its cars plunging, Chrysler had one

option: invest more than $200 million in designing, developing, and tooling models restyled under Exner's direction. The investment paid off with record sales in '55.

Advertised as the car "styled for tomorrow," the new DeSoto was lower, wider, and longer than before on a wheelbase stretched slightly to 126 inches. Even when resting, '55 DeSotos appeared to be in motion with their wraparound "New Horizon" windshield, aerodynamic hood ornament, and chrome-outlined contrasting color sweeps that were new for the year. Up front was a grinning grille of eight chromed teeth at the end of its sloped, rounded nose. The 55 color combinations on offer were coordinated

with interior color schemes (though the red-and-white cabin attire shown should have been black and white).

Enhancements to the interior were more than cosmetic. The gullwing-shaped dual-cockpit instrument panel included a glove compartment, radio, clock, courtesy lights, and the chrome-plated "Flite Control" shift lever for the PowerFlite transmission. Called the "finest completely automatic transmission available," the two-speed unit helped the driver navigate through traffic, rock out of snow or mud, brake down steep hills, and slip into tight parking spaces.

There were two series, the entry-level Firedome and a new premium line called Fireflite. Body styles available in both series included the two-door hardtop, four-door sedan, and convertible—and Firedome added a four-door station wagon to the mix.

In Firedomes, a 291-cid hemispherical-head V-8 engine with a two-barrel carburetor made 185 bhp, enough to propel them to speeds up to 100 mph, all on regular gas. Gone for good was the Powermaster series with its L-head six-cylinder engine.

All Series S-22 Firedome models were priced at less than $3200 without optional equipment like PowerFlite. Sixty-seven percent of the year's 115,485 DeSoto customers opted for Firedomes—but just 625 were convertibles.

1955
Ford Fairlane Sunliner Convertible Coupe

The U.S. auto industry's phenomenal year of 1955 found Ford in a familiar place: second to Chevrolet overall—but first in convertible sales. In a record-setting model year in which more than 7 million American passenger cars were built, the dramatically new Chevy drew more than 1.7 million orders, about 250,000 more than the 1,451,157 Fords produced. But, as they had done in most years since the convertible coupe style arrived on the scene, ragtop lovers flocked to Ford showrooms in '55. They took home 49,966 Fairlane Sunliners. Only Chevy came remotely close with about 41,000 soft-top sales.

Ford was fond of giving individual body styles their own names, and in 1952 it started calling convertibles Sunliners. The open car was then part of the high-line Crestline series, but for 1955 that moniker was dropped in favor of Fairlane, a title cribbed from the name of Henry Ford's estate in Dearborn, Michigan.

The '55 Fairlane lorded over a product line that sported dramatically new sheetmetal and a trendy wraparound windshield draped over the carryover 115.5-inch-wheelbase chassis. A concave checkerboard grille, "checkmark" bodyside trim (on Fairlanes), and large "Jet-Tube" taillights completed the look. Underneath, the front ball joints took on a slight rearward tilt to better absorb road shocks and all models now boasted 11-inch-diameter brake drums.

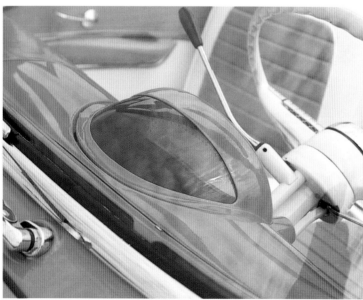

Interiors featured a new dash design that retained the see-through "Astra-Dial" speedometer concept first seen in 1954. Convertibles were trimmed with all-vinyl upholstery in five two-tone combinations, such as the rose-and-white ensemble perfectly suited to this Tropical Rose-over-Snowshoe White ragtop that came back to life following a six-year restoration. Their rayon tops could be had in a choice of black, blue, or tan.

Ford upgraded its year-old "Y-Block" ohv V-8 and improved the optional three-speed Ford-O-Matic automatic transmission. The engine was bored and stroked to grow from 239 to 272 cid. Horsepower in the two-barrel-carburetor version shown here came in at 162; a four-barrel carb and dual exhausts boosted output by 20 bhp. (The 292-cid V-8 from the new two-seat Thunderbird also became available for Fairlanes and station wagons.) Meanwhile, Ford-O-Matic became a little more flexible when it was modified to permit low-gear starts when the throttle was fully open. The 223-cid six, now at 120 bhp, was standard, as was a three-speed manual transmission.

1955
Hudson Hornet Hollywood Hardtop Coupe

oyalists who stuck with Hudson after its 1954 merger with Nash had to get used to some changes in their marque of choice. Consolidation of assembly in Nash plants spelled the end of Hudson's signature "Step-down" bodies. For 1955, they were replaced by Nash unitized bodies—albeit with some appearance modifications—available only in two-door hardtop and four-door sedan styles.

Hudson also shared Nash's shorter 114.25- and 121.25-inch wheelbases, switched to rear coil springs, and adopted some different powertrain features. Owners were introduced to Nash features like "Twin Travel Bed" seats and air conditioning with the works confined to under the hood.

However, Hudson partisans could still find familiar touchstones in these new cars, particularly in '55. Six-cylinder models continued to sport L-head Hudson-designed engines, including the 308-cid Hornet mill that made 170 bhp when equipped with the Twin H-Power dual-carburetor manifold. The "Triple Safe" brake system, a Hudson feature since 1936, was continued, too.

While Nash doors opened with a squeeze of their flat handles, entry to Hudsons still required gripping a loop-style handle and depressing a thumb button. The thick

grille frame incorporated parking/turn-signal lamps at its lower ends as in previous years; the grille's eggcrate surface came from a '55 Step-down facelift Hudson had in the works before the merger. Series-identification badges and the trunk ornament were carried over from '54, as were the instrument cluster, radio controls, and steering wheel.

What was new to both American Motors brands in 1955 was V-8 power, in this case a Packard-built 320-cid ohv engine with two-barrel carburetion rated at 208 bhp. Cars with this engine were hooked to Packard's Twin Ultramatic automatic transmission. The V-8 powerteam in a 121.25-inch-wheelbase Hudson Hornet added $255–$265 to the cost of a six-cylinder job with the standard three-speed manual transmission. As *Motor Trend* reported, the new powerplant delivered 0–60-mph acceleration in 12.1 seconds and a top speed of around 105 mph.

Thanks in part to an introduction that was delayed until February 1955, production of full-sized Hudsons tumbled by 44 percent from '54. Thus, deliveries of some models were particularly low. For instance, just 1770 Hornet Custom Hollywood V-8 hardtops were built.

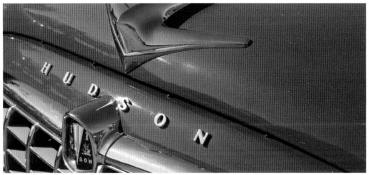

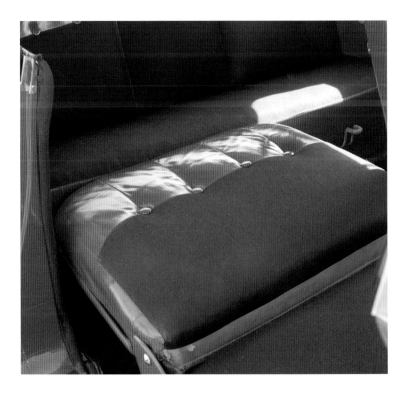

These redone Hornets abandoned the nameplate's days as a dominant force in stock-car racing, putting more emphasis on driving comfort. That was enhanced by things like the all-coil suspension and extra-cost power steering—a feature that *Motor Trend* heartily endorsed after testing a '55 Hudson without it. For convenience, there were options like power windows and the modern air conditioner that didn't require bulky components that robbed space from the trunk.

Bouncing back from a dismal 1954, overall Hudson sales increased by about 21 percent in '55, all thanks to compact Nash-designed Ramblers. But it was Nash that was doing most of the business for the new corporation, and as such there would be consequences. The distinctly Hudson elements of these hybrid "Hashes"—grille design, six-cylinder engines, etc.—started slipping away in 1956. Indeed, Hudson itself was rapidly fading, its name to be stricken from the roster of American automakers just a year later.

1955
Lincoln Capri
Convertible Coupe

The 1955 Lincolns were about as new as they could be, considering they came in body designs that already had three seasons on them. Aside from an obligatory touch-up of external details, the '55 Lincolns sported an all-new powertrain.

By boring out its ohv V-8 engine, Lincoln increased displacement from 317.5 cubic inches to 341. The extra cubes, a new high-lift camshaft, standard dual exhausts, and a half-point compression boost to 8.5:1 produced almost 10 percent more power than in '54. Thus, the "Fleet-Power" mill now made 225 bhp at 4400 rpm and 332

pound-feet of torque at 2500 rpm.

In place of the Hydra-Matic transmission Lincoln had been buying from General Motors, it now had its first homegrown automatic: Turbo-Drive. It consisted of a torque converter and three planetary gears, and offered the availability of low-gear starts if the accelerator was floored. The new powertrain propelled the two-ton-plus 1955 Lincoln to 60 mph in 12 seconds.

Frontal styling was freshened with a new grille made up of horizontal bars. Headlamps were newly hooded in period style. In back, the impression of length was enhanced via rear-leaning fender ends. Bodyside

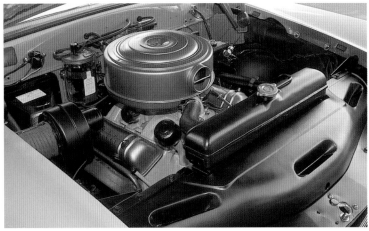

sculpting, which had risen high on the rear quarters of 1952–54 Lincolns, was now confined to the lower half of the body and pointed forcefully forward.

There were parts of the existing Lincoln package worth keeping. The 1955 models retained the prevailing 123-inch wheelbase and continued riding on an updated version of the ball-joint independent front suspension that won its predecessors raves for their handling.

In spite of the improvements, Lincoln suffered saleswise in 1955, which was a phenomenal year for the auto industry as a whole. At a time when year-to-year novelty was almost expected from automakers, a fourth-year design seemed old hat. Model-year production slumped to 27,222, a 26-percent drop from the year before. (Even the '52s, built under government-imposed production limits due to the Korean War, were more numerous—by 49 cars.)

Just 1487 of the '55s were convertibles from the upper-echelon Capri series. At $4072 to start, the convert-

ible was the costliest of the five Lincoln models cataloged for the year. Cashmere Coral was one of 14 exterior paint choices, and it could be coordinated with a Cashmere Coral-and-Ermine White interior. Leather upholstery was standard in convertibles.

The '55s marked the end of the road for the "Road Race Lincolns" that carved out a brilliant record of success in the Carrera Panamericana. Lincolns scored stock-class victories in the harsh trans-Mexico dash from 1952 to 1954.

1955
Oldsmobile 88
Two-Door Sedan

With the exceptions of some early compacts and a few two-seat sports cars, American automakers of the Fifties generally made one core product. There might be variances in chassis length, interior and exterior trim, and powertrains—but there was no mistaking that the least-expensive member of the family was kin to the costliest. You could see it in their faces—and maybe on the sides and back, too.

The middle of the decade was a high time for the numerous brands that served the medium-price segment. Theirs was a broad territory that started just above the Chevrolet/Ford/Plymouth boundary and stretched to a place a little short of the luxury marques. It was a group that counted Oldsmobile as its revered elder with a history that dated to 1897, and Olds was committed to covering much of this middle space as evidenced by its spare to sparkly lineup.

All 1955 Oldsmobiles—base 88, Super 88, and Ninety-Eight—were built off General Motors's corporate "B" body, with the Ninety-Eight making use of four additional inches of wheelbase and a rear deck that was five inches longer than on 88-class cars. Collectively, they formed a product portfolio with starting prices that ranged from $2297 to $3276. The 88 two-door sedan was at the very bottom of that spread.

To get to that level, which came quite close to the prices of some premium models from the "low-priced three" (and was actually higher than the cost of the ostensibly more upmarket Buick Special), the 88 had to leave a lot to the buyer's imagination. For instance, standard equipment did not include things like a clock, radio, or full wheel covers. The original purchaser of the example shown dug a little deeper to equip it with a Hydra-Matic automatic transmission; heater; and light package with underhood, trunk, and back-up lights. A dealer-effected repaint of the roof brought about the two-tone color scheme for $13.50, and an accessory exhaust extension cost all of 65 cents.

What, then, might have drawn shoppers to an Oldsmobile in '55? In the second year of a three-year body cycle, a deftly revised grille and side trim resulted in an attractive car. The 324.3-cid ohv "Rocket" V-8 had a quarter-point boost in compression ratio to 8.5:1 that increased the horsepower of the 88's two-barrel-carburetor engine from 170 to 185. The four-barrel powerplant that was standard in Super 88s and Ninety-Eights—and optional in 88s—saw horsepower jump from 185 to 202. Ride and handling were improved with a new front suspension dubbed "Power Ride" that replaced the previous lever-type shock absorbers with direct-action tubular shocks.

The public liked the combination of looks, performance, and value. Though just 37,507 of the 88 two-door sedans (and 11,950 similar Super 88s) were ordered—sportier hardtops being greatly preferred by buyers of two-door Oldses—overall production of 583,181 units for the model year was a division record that would stand for 10 years.

1956
Chevrolet One-Fifty
Two-Door Utility Sedan

The Chevrolets of 1955–57 have long been considered darlings among car enthusiasts for their iconic styling and legendary "small-block" V-8s. Typically for Fifties and Sixties collector cars, the most sought-after models are top-line, heavily-optioned convertibles and two-door hardtops. That's why most Chevrolet collectors fawn over glitzy, two-toned Bel-Airs festooned with an abundance of flashy factory accessories.

However, not every new Chevrolet shopper in the mid Fifties was swayed by fender skirts, bumper guards, tissue dispensers, signal-seeking radios, or Autronic Eye headlamp control. Some buyers just wanted to go as fast as possible for as little money as necessary, and were willing to forego creature comforts in the pursuit of speed. The age-old recipe for going fast on the cheap hasn't changed much over the years: Simply drop the hottest engine into the lightest, cheapest body available, and hold the frills. You are looking at a textbook example of the perfect budget bomb of its day.

With a 3110-pound shipping weight and an $1833 base price, the One-Fifty two-door utility sedan was the lightest and least-expensive V-8 Chevrolet offered in 1956. A single chrome side spear (a new embellishment for the series) and small hubcaps highlighted its austere exterior trim. Interior accouterments were equally Spartan: rubber floor mats; a single sun visor; and no radio, heater, or clock.

Rear side windows were fixed in place—who needs rolldown rear windows with no back seat? The utility sedan featured a 31-cubic-foot cargo area lined by "durable composition-board loadspace walls" behind the single split-bench seat. While most '56 Chevys were available in multiple interior color choices, One-Fifty sedan buyers had no options; a beige and gold-striped vinyl with golden-flecked black pattern cloth was the sole trim combination.

Just a year old, the Chevrolet V-8 was already well on its way to becoming a performance legend when the '56 models were introduced. A disguised 1956 Chevy prepared and driven by Corvette engineering guru Zora Arkus-Duntov set

a new Pikes Peak Hill Climb record on Labor Day 1955, and hot rodders were quickly discovering how well the new engine responded to performance modifications.

Chevrolet engineers did a little hot rodding of their own when the Corvette dual-four-barrel 265 was made available as an across-the-board option midway through the 1956 season. With the first of the famous "Duntov" cams, dual four-barrel carbs, lightweight valves, and larger intake and

exhaust ports, it was good for 225 bhp at 5200 rpm. The Carter carburetors were topped with a large "batwing" air cleaner from which hung two oil-bath air filters. It took about $200 to put one in a One-Fifty, and it could be paired with the extra-cost Powerglide automatic transmission.

Mechanix Illustrated's Tom McCahill hit 60 mph in 8.9 seconds and topped out at 120 mph driving a six-passenger One-Fifty with the twin-carb mill and standard stickshift.

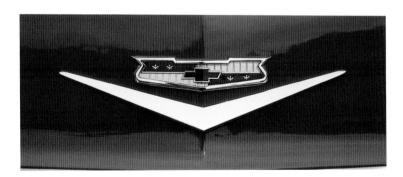

1956
Pontiac Star Chief Custom Safari Station Wagon

The first Pontiac Safari was destined to forever be overshadowed by its Chevrolet Nomad relative. In total 1955–57 production, the Nomad more than doubled the Safari, 22,375 units to 9094. In the collector market, the Nomad is better known and brings higher prices at auctions. Yet Safari is an interesting variation on the Nomad theme that deserves all the recognition it can get.

The high-style wagons sprang from a show car. For the 1954 General Motors Motorama, corporate styling chief Harley Earl asked for further body styles based on the new Chevrolet Corvette roadster. One concept was a sleek station wagon dubbed Nomad.

The show car proved popular at the Motorama, and Earl pushed to have it put into production. However, instead of a Corvette wagon, the production Nomad was part of the full-size Chevrolet line for '55. Corvettes were selling in small numbers; the two-door Nomad had a greater chance of success as a member of the premium Bel Air series.

To increase the wagon's chance of profitability, it was suggested that sharing body-production expenses with a Pontiac version would lead to greater volume and, therefore, to lower costs. That spawned the Safari.

The Nomad and Safari shared a distinctive two-door roof and transom-style tailgate, with sheetmetal below the beltline unique to each brand. Safari rode on a Pontiac chassis with a 122-inch wheelbase seven inches longer than the Nomad's span. The bigger Safari was 350 pounds heavier than a V-8 Nomad—which was also available with a six. To

move the extra weight, Safari had a bigger V-8. For 1956, the Pontiac engine grew to 316.6 cid while Chevy stuck to its 265-cid powerplant.

Reportedly, only 10 '56 Safaris were equipped with the standard manual transmission; the other 4032 had a Hydra-Matic automatic. An advantage for Safari was that the Hydra-Matic had four speeds, while Nomad's available Powerglide was a two-speed. With the automatic, the standard Safari V-8 developed 227 bhp. (About 200 Pontiacs were equipped with a race-ready 285-bhp engine and manual transmission, but it's not known how many, if any, were installed in Safaris.)

Safari was in Pontiac's top Star Chief Custom range and its interior was far more luxurious than Nomad's. Leather upholstery was a no-cost option, and a carpeted cargo floor was highlighted with stainless-steel strips. Nomad had nylon-and-vinyl upholstery, and its cargo floor was covered with linoleum.

As the 1955 Pontiacs were completely new, appearance changes for '56 weren't too drastic. There was a chromier grille, "gullwing" front bumper, and reoriented side trim. Headlight rims were body color, though the car shown sports '55 chromed rings. The '56s were the last Pontiacs to wear the brand's familiar "Silver Streak" hood trim.

Safari was admired as a stylish twist on the utilitarian station wagon with its low, hardtoplike styling and rakishly slanted, chrome-ribbed tailgate. At $3129, it was the costliest 1956 Pontiac, but it wasn't as convenient as four-door wagons. The two-door Safari was dropped after 1957, but the name lived on among conventional Pontiac wagons.

1956
Studebaker Golden Hawk Hardtop Coupe

Studebaker was struggling mightily in the mid Fifties, but if it had one thing going for it—apart from an infusion of Packard's money, which was no longer too plentiful—it was a particularly beautiful body for two-door models. That was the so-called "Loewy coupe" design done by Raymond Loewy employee Bob Bourke for the all-new line of 1953 Studebakers.

In 1954, Studebaker and Packard were merged, and the new S-P management decided it needed someone less expensive than the renowned Loewy to style its cars in the future. But while it turned over the styling of its 1956

sedans and station wagons to Vince Gardner, it gave Loewy's firm one last crack at facelifting the stunning coupes and hardtops it had created. The result was a series of four cars in a new family of Hawks. The most prestigious of them all was the Golden Hawk.

In place of the drooping hood and low grille of the 1953–55 Studes, Bourke substituted a taller hood that tapered back from a trapezoidal central grille. Horizontal slots flanking the grille bore hints of the previous design, though. In back, the rounded decklid of the past was updated with a flat, ribbed section to which further attention was called

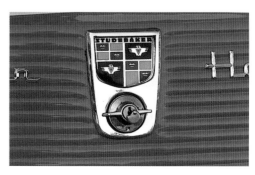

via the use of contrast-color paint on two-tone cars. Low-line Flight and Power Hawks utilized the pillared roofline of the 1953–55 Starlight coupes, but lusher Sky and Golden Hawks adopted the related Starliner pillarless hardtop roof.

The Golden Hawk's emblems of rank began with tailfins. Vertical fiberglass blades were grafted atop the rear quarter panels. (Though fairly modest for the era, Bourke didn't care for the car's fins.) Wheel-arch moldings linked by ribbed lower-body trim also distinguished the Golden Hawk, as did a wide bright band at the rear of the roof.

While lesser Hawks were powered by Studebaker-built six-cylinder and V-8 engines, the Golden Hawk received Packard's 352-cid V-8. With 275 bhp on tap, the engine could propel the Golden Hawk to top speeds of more than 120 mph. A three-speed manual transmission was standard, with overdrive and Packard's Twin-Ultramatic automatic available.

The power and panache sold for $3061 without any options. Orders totaled 4071 for 1956. The most gilded of Studebaker's Hawks remained in production until 1958.

1957
Buick Century
Convertible Coupe

Twenty-one years after its introduction, the Buick Century was still playing its historic role as a "banker's hot rod." The Century series bowed in '36 when Buick dropped its biggest engine in a smaller chassis. Thanks to the resulting power-to-weight ratio, the Century name was no idle boast: By its second season, the car could do 100 mph. Retired after 1942, the Century was returned to the line from 1954 through 1958.

The same essential formula was still in play in 1957, when the Century shared its 122-inch wheelbase with the entry-level Special but had the more powerful engine of the larger Super and Roadmaster models. *Motor Life* estimated a top speed well beyond the Century mark at 125 mph.

All '57 Buicks had a 364-cid ohv V-8 as a replacement for the prior 322-cubic-inch engine. In the case of the Century and the "senior" Buicks, a four-barrel carburetor and 10.0:1 compression ratio produced 300 bhp—a 50-horsepower advantage over the Special—with 330 ponies optionally on tap. By comparison, the standard Cadillac engine of that same year also put out 300 bhp, yet was only one cubic inch larger. To make the most of that additional power, Buick had recently improved its smooth, but formerly sluggish, Dynaflow automatic transmission for faster acceleration. With this powerteam, *Motor Trend* timed the 0–60-mph sprint in a 1957 Century at 10.1 seconds.

Meanwhile, handling was better thanks to a lower ride height and Buick's first ball-joint front suspension—though "better" is a relative term as this was a Fifties Buick with a suspension tuned more for a soft boulevard ride than sports car handling. The "newest Buick yet" (as advertising proclaimed) also rested on a new X-braced perimeter frame and incorporated an extra universal joint in the driveline, which lowered the transmission tunnel.

Buick had new bodies for '57 that were longer and lower, yet carried over the styling themes of recent years—such as fender "portholes," dramatic bodyside "sweepspear"

trim, and the return of a vertical-bar grille—to maintain continuity. Just in case the changes were so subtle that one didn't recognize a new Buick, the badge on the center of the grille proudly proclaimed "1957."

Centurys came in five body styles that made use of General Motors's B-body shells. The 4085 Century convertibles built weighed 4234 pounds and cost $3598 in standard trim. However, those numbers could rise with the inclusion of options like a Sonomatic radio that could be tuned via a floor pedal to seek the next station and power assists for brakes, steering, front seat, and windows.

1957
Chevrolet Bel Air Convertible Coupe

For a variety of reasons, some of them not always clearly understood or acknowledged, the 1957 Chevrolet has become the avatar for the popular notion of the American automobile of the Fifties. Without a doubt, the fullest expression of the '57 Chevy is the peacock of the line, the brightly trimmed and amply equipped Bel Air.

The Bel Air name shot to prominence during the decade, starting out as the label for Chevrolet's two-door hardtop in 1950. Then, it was bestowed onto a full series of plusher-than-ever Chevys in 1953. Four years later, the Bel Air line consisted of seven body styles: sedans and hardtops each in a choice of two or four doors; a Townsman four-door station wagon; the rakish Nomad two-door wagon; and a convertible. The '57s flaunted their rank with a wide fan of ribbed and anodized bright metal on the rear quarters, plus a grille surface, hood and trunk badges, and front-fender chevrons all in a gold tone. Base prices ranged from $2238 for two-door sedan with the "Blue Flame" six to $2857 for a V-8 Nomad.

In 1957, the year in which the Bel Air series became Chevy's best seller for the first time, 47,562 convertibles

found homes. Sierra Gold was one of 16 solid paint colors buyers could choose (four more than other Bel Airs). They coordinated with seven interior combinations and fabric tops available in Ivory, Black, Light Blue, Medium Green, or Tan Beige, depending on body color. Owners could dress them up with options like power window lifts, a power seat,

power radio antenna, windshield washer, "Wonder Bar" signal-seeking radio, spinner-hub wheel covers, and a Continental kit spare-tire carrier.

The general layout of the 1957 Chevrolet wasn't far removed from that of the '55 model that changed the brand's public image. Underhood, however, the brilliant "small-block" V-8 was enlarged to 283 cubic inches. (The original 265-cube version remained available as the base V-8.) Horsepower ratings of the 283 started at 185 with a two-barrel carburetor and rose through 220 with a four-barrel, 245 and 270 with twin four-pot carbs, and 250 or 283—the magic of one horsepower per cubic inch of displacement—with Rochester mechanical fuel injection. The 270- and 283-horsepower engines used solid valve lifters while the others had hydraulic tappets.

Also new was a second automatic-transmission option, the smooth but complex triple-turbine Turboglide. Then, too,

the fine roadability of the 1955-generation Chevrolets was improved via a stiffer frame and wider spacing for the rear leaf springs.

Although the 1957 Chevrolet is cherished by collectors today, in its day it was outsold by Ford for the model year while Plymouth made big gains with its trend-setting styling —both had new designs while Chevy was in the third year of a styling cycle. However, it did get a considerable facelift that included a new grille-and-bumper combo and pointed rear-quarter extensions suggestive of the era's trendy tailfins. The hood and cowl were lowered, and Chevrolets were 1.5 inches lower altogether, in part due to a switch to smaller 14-inch-diameter wheels. Inside, there was a new dashboard with a radio speaker moved from the right side to the center top for better sound quality. Though it couldn't beat Ford in sales, the inherent goodness of this Chevy— especially the Bel Air—made it a collectible for the ages.

1957
Dodge Coronet Texan Hardtop Coupe

Dodge shed a stodgy image once and for all with its daring "swept wing" styling of 1957. The cars were lower and fins were higher. Windshields wrapped well above the front doors and there was so much glass that one wondered what supported the low-profile roof. Instead of a conventional grille, parallel chrome beams formed a huge bumper/grille.

The only place where Dodge played it safe was with the headlights. Three U.S. states hadn't yet approved quad headlights by '57, so large parking

lights were mounted inboard of the hooded headlights to suggest the quad-headlight look, while remaining legal in every state. Stacked dual taillights at the rear presented no such regulatory worries, and they furthered a Dodge styling idea that had been in use since 1955.

While everyone was taken with Chrysler styling director Virgil Exner's "Forward Look," there was also a major technical innovation: Torsion-bar front suspension would be a trademark of Chrysler Corporation cars long after tailfins were gone. Chrysler claimed the longitudinal torsion bars gave a better ride than conventional coil springs, yet the '57s also handled better than any previous Dodge—and better than the competition.

Power came from a six (restricted to entry-level Coronets) and five V-8s, ranging from 138 to 340 bhp. The most powerful were the D-500 V-8s with efficient, domed "hemi" combustion chambers in their heads. The 325-cid Super D-500 with dual four-barrel carbs (shown) put out 310 bhp.

Regional marketing is no new idea, as evidenced by the Texan model. Available through Dodge dealers in the Lone

Star State, Texans were based on the custom-trimmed Coronet four-door sedan, hardtop sedan, hardtop coupe, and two-door club sedan. (A convertible was added in '58.) The custom interior was a bit more luxurious than that found in base Coronets. Special Texan badges were added to the glovebox door, the tailfins, and the trunklid, where on the example depicted it took the place of a tag that would have announced the presence of the D-500—a spot unlucky challengers would have been sure to see it.

1957
Pontiac Star Chief Hardtop Coupe

T he 1957 Pontiac was the first Pontiac since 1934 without "Silver Streaks" on the hood. Before Cadillac had tailfins and Buick had portholes, Pontiac had its signature chrome band (or bands) atop the hood. However, Semon E. "Bunkie" Knudsen arrived as the division's new general manager just as the '57 models were ready for production, and he was determined to change that.

Pontiac's position in the industry had been slipping. Knudsen believed a fresher, more youthful image was needed. Removing the Silver Streaks was seen as a break with the past—and a tradition that started while Knudsen's father, William S. Knudsen, was running Pontiac. It was also about the only change he could reasonably make at so late a date.

Actually, Pontiac's transformation from an "old man's car" had started in 1955. Pontiac shared Chevrolet's "A" body, which was restructured for '55. That year's Pontiacs were lower, sleeker, and more modern than before. Just as Chevrolet had a new ohv V-8 for '55, so did Pontiac. In fact, the Chevy engine's effective valve gear with lightweight, stamped rocker arms was borrowed from designs developed in Pontiac's engineering department. Pontiac's V-8 proved long-lived and versatile. The basic design lasted until the division stopped building its own V-8s in 1981, supporting displacements from 287 to 455 cubic inches.

The new V-8 cars had far more performance than the old straight-eight Pontiacs. To demonstrate the newfound power, Bonneville Salt Flats legend Ab Jenkins was recruited to set a world record. In his hands, a 1956 Pontiac averaged 118.375 mph for 24 hours.

Bunkie Knudsen wanted to foster a performance image for Pontiac. Advertising in 1957 proclaimed it "America's Number 1 Road Car." Backing up that claim, Pontiac grew its V-8 to 347 cid, which helped it deliver from 227 to 317 bhp. Styling was also more exciting for 1957, even if still on the underlying '55 bodies.

Since 1954, a longer-wheelbase/stretched-deck series called Star Chief sat at the head of Pontiac's table. For '57 it came in eight variations, including the Bonneville, a new and rare deluxe convertible with a fuel-injected engine. Pontiac dubbed its hardtop models Catalinas, and Custom-trim versions of the 1957 Star Chiefs featured a fetching "off-the-shoulder" design for seats upholstered in leather and fabric or all leather in four color combinations. The 32,862 two-door Star Chief Custom Catalinas built started at $2901, but a Hydra-Matic transmission cost extra.

In spite of a good product, Pontiac sales were down for '57. Knudsen's efforts wouldn't truly start to bear fruit until 1959 when the "Wide Track" Pontiac rose to number four in sales.

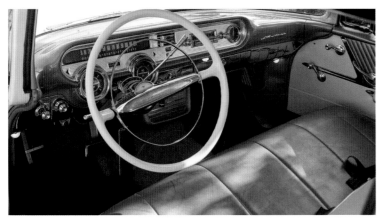

1958
Buick Century
Caballero Station Wagon

The "hardtop convertible" concept ran through the auto industry like wildfire in the Fifties. Originally conceived for two-door models, it came to include four-door cars by mid decade, and then spread to station wagons that likewise did away with fixed B-pillars.

However, while hardtop coupes and sedans went on to enjoy more than two decades on the automotive scene, hardtop wagons lasted only about one third as long. Nash and Hudson Ramblers were the first of the breed in 1956; Chryslers and Dodge Custom 880s brought the idea to its conclusion in 1964.

Buick was involved up to its neck in the hardtop trend. The 1949 Roadmaster Riviera was one of the three General Motors models that first brought the hardtop-coupe body style to market. Six years later, the Special and Century (and the B-body Oldsmobiles) pioneered the four-door hardtop sedan. Then, come 1957, Buick entered the quickly expanding hardtop-wagon arena—Oldsmobile and Mercury were other newcomers.

A brace of hardtop haulers issued from Flint, the Special Riviera Estate Wagon and the Century Caballero on a shared 122-inch wheelbase. Each was powered and equipped to match the sedans, hardtops, and convertible in their respective series, though the Caballero was augmented with a group of nine thin chrome strips on the rear half of its roof that its Special running mate lacked.

The duo continued into 1958, when a considerable reworking of external sheetmetal was executed over

carryover inner bodies. New quad headlights sat under flaring fender caps and peered over a full-width "Fashion-Aire Dynastar Grille" composed of 160 dimpled chrome knobs. In a backward step, after years of trying to lower hoods, the hood on 1958 Buicks once again sat higher than the fender tops. Slight chrome-capped fins rose over the rear quarter panels, which ended in stout upright taillight bezels and a massive bumper. The marque's signature "ventiports" were dropped, but there probably wasn't room for them anyway amid the welter of brightwork applied to the bodysides.

To the chassis changes instituted for 1957, Centurys like the Caballero now added standard air-cooled and finned aluminum front brake drums with cast-iron linings for rapid heat dissipation. These binders completely turned around Buick's recent reputation for substandard braking.

Rated output of the 364-cid V-8 held at 300 bhp, but torque was increased to 400 pound-feet. It was hooked to a "Variable-Pitch Dynaflow" automatic transmission, but a more complex triple-turbine "Flight-Pitch" variant with even greater torque-multiplication potential was newly available.

Opening the Caballero's two-piece tailgate—with a wide, wraparound transom—exposed a carpeted cargo floor. The Buick wagons were six-place vehicles, but the Century could be ordered with a rear-facing third seat for two or three extra passengers. Other available wagon add-ons were a rare split-folding back seat and a roof rack.

Caballeros always outsold the cheaper Special Riviera Estates, but demand for both tumbled in recessionary 1958. Only 4456 Century haulers priced at $3831 were built that year, the last of Buick's hardtop station wagons.

1958
Edsel Bermuda Station Wagon

Ford had its Country Squire, Mercury had its Colony Park, and when Edsel made its debut for 1958, it would have its own deluxe station wagon. Edsel called it the Bermuda and, like its counterparts from the other Ford Motor Company divisions, it stood out at a glance due to its simulated wood trim.

The public buildup for the Edsel—a publicity campaign more than a year in the making—led consumers to believe the corporation's new medium-price make would be nothing less than a radical departure in automobiles. But when the wraps finally came off on September 4, 1957, the only truly unconventional feature of the car was its styling.

Edsel immediately ran nose-first into controversy with its vertical central grille that detractors came to call the "horse collar." Meanwhile, in terms of engineering, the 1958 Edsels owed practically everything to the Fords and Mercurys from which they were derived. When that realization sank in with car shoppers, the bloom was off the rose.

The Edsel Corsair and Citation shared bodies with Mercurys, but had their own wheelbase and 410-cid version of the V-8s developed for Lincolns and Mercs. The price-leader Ranger and step-up Pacer not only borrowed

body shells from Ford's Fairlanes, but had the same 118-inch wheelbase.

Like some other manufacturers at the time, Edsel treated its station wagons as a separate series. Two- and four-door Villagers were trimmed to match the Rangers. Four-door Bermudas got the slightly plusher Pacer interior. But they all had the same basic bodies and 116-inch wheelbase of Ford wagons. (The wood tones on the featured car are close to those found on Country Squires and Colony Parks, but actual Bermuda trim was a lighter, grayish shade called Driftwood.)

FoMoCo launched the "FE" series of V-8 engines in '58. The largest, a 361-cid job, was reserved for the junior Edsels. Billed as the "E-400" (for its torque output), it made 303 bhp. A three-speed manual transmission was standard; overdrive and a "Teletouch" three-speed automatic operated by push buttons in the steering-wheel hub could be ordered.

The Bermuda seen here optioned with the automatic transmission, dual exhausts, and twin external mirrors is one of 1456 six-passenger models made. Another 779 came with seating for nine.

1958
Cadillac Eldorado
Seville Hardtop Coupe

W hat began as a limited attempt by Cadillac to offer a customized buzz generator in the vein of the Buick Skylark and Oldsmobile Fiesta turned out to have long-lasting consequences. From 1953 to 1966 the Eldorado was Caddy's convertible flagship, but it did pair with a hardtop-coupe companion from 1956 through 1960.

In most of those years, Eldorados relied on extra chrome, slightly more horsepower, and a plusher interior to justify the price premium they held over their Series 62 and De Ville counterparts. However, for a few years starting in '55, Eldorado was further distinguished by unique rear sheet-metal, and for 1957–58 the back half of the car was even more distinctive by dint of slim tailfins that rose out of a rounded, sloping tail above an elaborate divided bumper.

When the Eldo added a second body style, it behooved Cadillac to give both their own names. Thus, the convertible was called Biarritz while the new two-door hardtop was

chrome-plated aluminum center, and the better air flow of their open-spoke design improved braking. The Seville continued to welcome lucky passengers onto seats covered in luxurious textured cloth and leather, and the roof was covered in a leatherlike vinyl-coated material. Available options ran to things like a power trunk release, Autronic-Eye automatic high-beam headlights, air conditioning, and trouble-prone air suspension.

The 335-bhp 365-cid V-8 bestowed on Eldorados was fed through triple two-barrel carburetors and made 25 more horsepower than the base engine with one four-barrel carb. Cadillac's Hydra-Matic transmission was similarly smooth. It had been upgraded in '56 with a second fluid coupling.

The starting price for Eldorados climbed to $7500 for 1958, a recession year in which nearly all automakers lost ground. Only 815 Biarritzes and 855 Sevilles were sold.

christened the Seville. At first, the Seville solidly outsold the Biarritz (though they sold for the same price), but by 1959 the open car had gained the upper hand.

Totally redesigned 1957 Cadillacs were mounted on a new X-member chassis that not only lowered them by three inches, but was more rigid. However, the new frame lacked side rails and was more vulnerable to side impacts. The '58s stuck to this platform and the new bodies that came with it, albeit with a thorough facelift. Quad headlights and a full-width grille highlighted with 80 small aluminum "bullets" constituted the new look. On the Eldorados, stylist Ron Hill's declining deck was carried over with little more than a shuffle of trunklid badging and different detailing of the bumper ends. Meanwhile, a series of nine chrome louvers was added ahead of the rear wheel opening.

Still standard on Eldos, and optional on other models, were "Sabre-Spoke" wheels. They had a steel rim with a

1959
Chrysler New Yorker Hardtop Coupe

The smartly elegant "Forward Look" offered by Chrysler Corporation for 1955–56 hurtled into '57 with enough aesthetic force to turn Detroit auto design on its ear. What had been the frumpiest of the Big Three was suddenly the industry's design leader. Company offerings for 1957 were delta-shaped in profile: low, lean, and swoopy.

In a Detroit era when show cars had names like Predictor and Nucleon, the new Chrysler products really did have an aura of futurism. Plymouth advertising that shouted, "Suddenly, it's 1960!" sounded like understatement.

For the period, these Chrysler vehicles were restrained and carried the new look well. Form didn't exactly follow function, but on most models the great fantails of fins didn't appear tacked on, either. In fact, corporate styling chief Virgil Exner tried to make the case that the fins seen on his 1957 creations actually played a hand in improving directional stability. Chrome and side trim were reasonably simple, too.

At Chrysler Division, the New Yorker had been the top of the line off and on since just before World War II, and

unquestionably held down that position in the late Fifties because the Imperial had been spun off as a freestanding luxury-class marque for 1955. Although the '57s gave the impression of great length, they actually were a bit shorter than the 1956 models while riding on the same 126-inch wheelbase.

For 1957 and '58, the New Yorker ran with a 392-cid "hemi" V-8 producing 325 or 345 bhp. The hemi had a heavy mystique, but it was expensive to produce, so for 1959 Chrysler fitted the New Yorker with a 413-cid V-8 sporting wedge-shaped combustion chambers, a four-barrel carburetor, 4.18×3.75-inch bore and stroke, and a 10.0:1 compression ratio. The motor lacked only the hemi allure; in power it was that engine's equal and more, producing a thumping 350 horses at 4600 rpm and 470 pound-feet of torque at 2800. The sole transmission was an excellent three-speed TorqueFlite automatic.

The '59 hardtop coupe had some physical substance, weighing in at 4080 pounds but able, nonetheless, to sprint from zero to 60 in approximately 10 seconds. Top speed was 115 mph.

Front suspension brought upper A-arms, lower traverse arms, longitudinal torsion bars, and an antiroll bar. Out back was a live axle and semielliptic leaf springs. Brakes, front and rear, were drums.

On the highway, these cars were smooth, powerful performers with spacious, airy interiors, and gave away little to Cadillac, Lincoln, or Imperial. Available comfort and luxury extras included things like power windows and air conditioning, plus a new and invariably interesting option: front swivel seats that could be rotated towards the open door to ease entry and exit.

Most every design element became a bit more baroque for 1958 and even more so for 1959—by which time Ford and General Motors had introduced imposing, swoopy cars of their own. The '59s showed heftier bumpers and headlamps were partially blended into the grille, a step towards the look that was already changing the face of the American car. The rear-end treatment displayed sharply pointed tailfin tips that loomed over stunted taillight lenses.

In 1959, a New Yorker hardtop coupe went out the door for $4476—up from $4347 in 1958 and $4202 in '57. Unfortunately, indifferent workmanship and a tendency to rust meant that the so-so sales figures for the 1957 Chrysler line only got worse for '58 and '59. Some 8863 New Yorker two-door hardtops were produced for 1957. For '58, the total fell to 3205 (due partly to the serious economic recession) and suffered another tumble for '59, when just 2435 units were produced.

1959
Mercury Colony Park Station Wagon

The 1959 Mercury should have been more popular. Redesigned for the second time in three years, Ford Motor Company's medium-price mainstay offered the biggest, smoothest, roomiest cars in its 20-year history, plus new features, better handling, and arguably nicer styling. Model-year production did grow some to exactly 150,000 units. However, in its segment, only Chrysler, DeSoto, and ill-starred Edsel fared worse.

What happened? Basically, General Motors' rival Buick, Oldsmobile, and Pontiac lines were unexpectedly redesigned—and in dramatic fashion, too. Though all three improved on their mediocre '58 sales, the handsome Wide-Track Pontiac was the big winner, jumping from sixth to fourth in the industry race on substantially higher volume

of almost 383,000 units. Mercury, meanwhile, slipped a notch to ninth.

Even so, the '59 "Big M" had plenty to offer. For starters, it was four inches longer, four inches wider, and three to four inches longer in wheelbase—increases made so that the powertrain could sit lower and more forward in a "cowbelly" frame with siderails spread farther apart. These changes resulted in a cavernous "Space-Planned" interior with a lower center tunnel, much-improved foot room, and easier entry/exit. The revised frame also allowed wider tracks for better cornering stability.

Compound-curve "Panoramic Skylight" windshields enhanced the airy interior feel, and their expansive glass area was effectively cleared of rain and snow by "Safety-

Sweep" windshield wipers—the industry's first parallel-acting wipers. A new slim-section dashboard grouped gauges and controls ahead of the driver. Styling was crisper and more conservative, with pie-wedge taillamps and large, rocket-shaped bodyside sculpting the only holdovers from the "dream car" spaciness of 1957–58.

Engine choices again comprised 312- and 383-cid V-8s, plus a Lincoln 430 as standard and exclusive to Park Lane. All were detuned for slightly better fuel economy after the 1957–58 recession led many car buyers to grumble about gas guzzlers. The available three-speed Merc-O-Matic transmission had a new companion in a more-flexible dual-range Multi-Drive unit. Both automatics were controlled by a conventional steering-column lever instead of push buttons, another retreat from dream-car gimmickry.

Mercury dropped its slow-selling entry-level "Medalist" (a name that never appeared on the car) and gaudy Turnpike Cruiser models for '59, leaving Monterey, Montclair, and luxury Park Lane hardtops, sedans, and convertibles. There were four station wagons, all with pillarless hardtop styling. Mercury claimed they held up to 101.1 cubic feet of cargo.

Colony Park remained the top-line wagon, trimmed and equipped to roughly Montclair level and set apart externally by pseudo-wood body paneling. Apart from its 1964 wheel covers, the one seen here is a fine example of a Colony Park in all its original glory with the standard 322-bhp 383-cube V-8, automatic transmission, and power-retracting tailgate window. Options include a front-facing third-row seat that could now fold into the floor. Only 5929 of the $3932 cars were built—still a sales increase from '58.

1959
Oldsmobile Dynamic 88 Holiday Hardtop Coupe

For 1959, General Motors originally planned to field a lineup of facelifted 1958 models. Designer Chuck Jordan's lunchtime discovery of '57 Plymouths sporting Chrysler's trendsetting "Forward Look" design one day in August 1956 changed all of that. The resulting chain of events culminated in the 1959 GM offerings that are now some of the most memorable cars of the Fifties.

Oldsmobile marketers dubbed the new styling the "Linear Look." While significantly bigger, the '59 Olds appeared leaner and cleaner than the overchromed 1958 model. Up front, parking lamps were placed between headlamp pairs newly lowered to each end of a full-width grille. Tall, narrow letters spelled out "OLDSMOBILE" in the middle of the grille, and the hood dropped down at the center. The clean flanks were topped at the beltline with a long nacelle in place of the expected tailfin. Both of these long booms terminated in an oval-shaped taillamp that suggested a rocket's exhaust.

Inside, occupants found a larger interior with greatly increased glass area. Passengers sat on "Fashion-Firm" seats—the front of which could be adjusted six ways via a power control. When drivers weren't looking out through the "Vista-Panoramic" windshield, they were probably consulting the "Safety-Spectrum" speedometer. Upon reaching their destination, "Easi-Grip" release levers opened the doors. At Oldsmobile, the riot of marketing jargon so associated with Fifties cars also described such available features as "Roto-Matic" power steering and "Pedal-Ease" power brakes.

Oldsmobile offered three series: low-price Dynamic 88, mid-level Super 88, and top-shelf Ninety-Eight. All featured a new "Guard-Beam" frame that combined elements of X-type and perimeter construction. Olds claimed the "Wide-Stance" chassis was sturdier than previous designs, helped reduce vibration, and provided a quieter "Glide" ride. The two 88 lines shared a 123-inch wheelbase, while Ninety-Eights rode a 126.3-inch span.

Oldses came in six body styles, but Dynamic 88 was the only series to have them all. The $2837 two-door sedan was the price leader, and the Celebrity sedan was the most-affordable four-door model. There were two Holiday hardtops: two-door SceniCoupe and four-door SportSedan. A convertible and the four-door Fiesta station wagon rounded out the choices. The Dynamic 88 SceniCoupe was the marque's most popular hardtop coupe. Its 40,259 orders outsold the Super 88 and Ninety-Eight two-doors combined.

The '59 Dynamic 88 had a 371-cid "Rocket" V-8 that was rated at 270 bhp with the standard "Econ-o-way" two-barrel carburetor, or 300 with the extra-cost four-barrel carb. A three-speed manual transmission was standard, but the optional "Jetaway" Hydra-Matic automatic transmission was found on most cars.

1960
Chrysler 300-F Convertible Coupe

Nineteen sixty was a year of change for Chrysler Corporation and the Chrysler 300 series. All Chrysler Corporation cars—except for the Imperial—switched to unibody construction. The Chryslers wore fresh styling, and the thundering 300-F's new design included a "cross-hair" grille that became a trademark touch for the remainder of the run of the "letter-series" cars to 1965.

Not as long-lived was the "Flight-Sweep Deck Lid," a spare-tire impression on the trunklid that was standard on the 300-F, but was dropped the next year. Also short-lived were the 300-F's front and rear bucket seats, a distinctive and sporty configuration that ended when the 300-J of 1963 reverted to a bench seat in back.

All '60 Chryslers had an innovative "AstraDome" instrument cluster that grouped the instruments under a clear hemispherical dome. Electroluminescent lighting cast a soft, green glow that made a memorable impression on those lucky enough to drive or ride in a 1960–62 Chrysler at night. Unfortunately, there was no place under the AstraDome for the 300-F's tachometer—a new feature for the year—which was located low on the center console where many complained that it was hard to read.

No one complained about the "Ram-Injection" V-8. The 413-cid V-8 introduced for 1959 replaced the earlier "hemi" mill's complex heads and valve gear with more conventional hardware. For 1960, the 413 gained a ram-induction intake manifold with 30-inch-long ram-intake tubes and

dual four-barrel carbs that sat on opposite sides of the engine.

Chrysler said the long tubes provided a "supercharger" effect without the complication of forced induction. The result was 375 bhp, meaning the 413 lost five horsepower compared to the 1959 version. But the revised powerplant gained 45 pound-feet of torque for a total of 495 pound-feet at 2800 rpm. This engine was linked to a standard TorqueFlite pushbutton automatic transmission.

There was also an extremely rare 400-horse version of the 300-F's 413 with modified intake tubes, mechanical valve lifters, and manual chokes for the carbs. Essentially purpose-built for a select few hotshoes seeking to set records on the sands of Daytona Beach, Florida, at the annual NASCAR Speed Weeks,

cars so equipped also had a French Pont-a-Mousson four-speed floor-shift manual gearbox.

Hot Rod magazine tested a 300-F hardtop coupe with the 375-bhp engine and automatic. Editor Ray Brock claimed, "The acceleration for a car of such weight borders on the fantastic." *Hot Rod* recorded a 0–60-mph time of 7.4 seconds, and the quarter-mile was covered in 16.0 seconds at 90.9 mph. As for its suspension with stiffer springs than other Chryslers, *Hot Rod* said, "At high speed through twisting mountain passes or over undulating desert dips, the 300-F is head and shoulders above any other car on the road."

Toreador Red was one of four colors available for the 300 in '60. The convertible started at a hefty $5841; it accounted for just 248 of a series total 1212 cars.

1960
Edsel Ranger
Two-Door Sedan

ntroduced by the Ford Motor Company in September 1957, Edsel was Ford's attempt to capture a larger portion of the market for medium-price cars. But by the beginning of the 1960 model year, the brand was on very shaky ground.

As the medium-price market developed in the years between the world wars, Ford really didn't do anything to address this growing—and profitable—part of the business. The 1939 Mercury was the company's first medium-price offering, but it had to compete with Pontiac, Oldsmobile, and Buick from General Motors; Dodge, DeSoto, and Chrysler from Chrysler; and a collection of strong independents including Nash and Hudson.

Ford executives recognized the importance of this market soon after the end of World War II. Still, serious strategic planning didn't begin until the Fifties.

Carefully orchestrated leaks and media speculation preceded the introduction of FoMoCo's new marque, destined to bow as a 1958 entry and positioned between Ford and Mercury. Despite the planning and hoopla, the Edsel faced major problems even before it ever went on sale.

The new car found itself caught up in a perfect storm of brutal office politics, a dramatic sales downturn in the medium-price field, and the worst economic conditions since the end of World War II. With sales failing to live up to expectations from the start, and powerful opponents in company management, Edsel quickly lost support inside of Ford, even before New Year's Day 1958. It was branded a loser, but no matter how good or bad the '58 Edsel truly was, it probably never really had a chance to succeed.

Edsel offerings were dramatically scaled back for 1959, and by 1960 the Edsel clearly was little more than a badge-engineered Ford. Unique sheetmetal was at a minimum, with the hood and the tops of the rear quarter-panels next to the decklid being the differences. Edsel's signature central vertical grille was jettisoned for a new front end reminiscent of a '59 Pontiac. At the rear, vertical taillamps set the car apart from the 1960 Ford with its horizontal lenses.

Introduced on October 15, 1959, the '60 Edsel arrived in one series, Ranger. There were two- and four-door sedans and hardtops, a convertible, and six- and nine-passenger Villager station wagons.

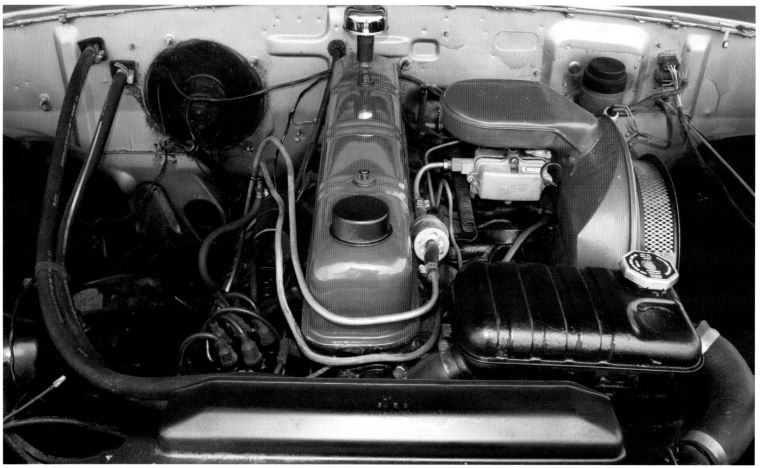

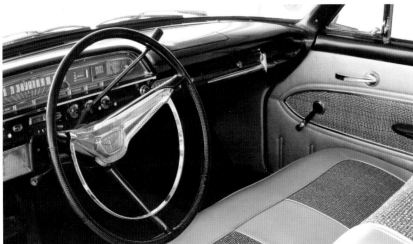

Dealer and customer response was tepid, allowing the company to officially throw in the towel on Edsel a little more than a month after the 1960 model's introduction. Production ended by November 30, 1959, and totaled a mere 2846 units.

Among the final Edsels, the two-door sedan was the price leader of the line at $2643 to start—and it got cheaper when ordered with the 145-bhp 223-cid "Econ-O-Six" engine. This new alternative to the standard 292-cube "Ranger V-8" was an $83.70 credit option. The two-door sedan turned out to be the second-most popular 1960 Edsel with a run of 777 units.

1960
Ford Galaxie Sunliner Convertible

Fords were drastically restyled for 1960. The brand's all-new "standards"—a qualifier that was especially necessary now that it was also making the personal-luxury Thunderbird and the compact Falcon—dropped every comfortably familiar marque styling cue of recent years. Instead, Ford went to a low, wide design topped off by trendy horizontal tailfins.

A broad grille that newly incorporated the quad headlights clearly demonstrated that the Fifties were over. The '60 Ford is said to have the widest hood of any American production car—helped by the fact that it extends almost to the edge of the fenders. Meanwhile, the usual circular taillights were abandoned for roughly semicircular lenses set at either end of a concave body cove. Closed cars were topped by glassy "greenhouses" that Ford said had up to 31 percent more glass area than before. Reverse-slant "dogleg" windshield pillars, a faddish but not particularly convenient feature of recent years, were replaced by forward-leaning pillars that eased entry and exit.

The look had originated as an advanced-design project dubbed "Quicksilver." When company chieftains warmed to it—by some accounts after being tipped off that rival Chevrolet was going to sweeping "batwing" fins for '59—the concept was ticketed to be the 1960 Ford.

The result was a car that was 5.6 inches longer (at 213.6 inches) and 4.9 inches wider (at 81.5 inches) than the popular 1959 Ford. In fact, that width was illegal in some states and was narrowed for 1961. Wheelbase grew one inch to 119 inches. Though the Quicksilver had been expected to rest on an all-new chassis, the production '60 Ford actually used a modified version of the marque's existing platform.

The 1960 full-size Ford line started with the fleet-market Custom 300. Regular retail offerings rose from the Fairlane to the Fairlane 500 and then the five-car Galaxie series. A station wagon group featured cars in three trim levels.

The only 1960 convertible was the $2860 Galaxie Sunliner—the slow-selling Skyliner retractable hardtop that

was perhaps born 40 years too soon having been discontinued after 1959. The Galaxie name was nowhere to be seen on the Sunliner and thin-pillar Starliner two-door hardtop, but both were trimmed and outfitted like all other top-series models.

The Sunliner shown here is awash in options and accessories like bumper guards with black-rubber inserts, exhaust tips, hood ornament, tissue dispenser, seatbelts, and dual rear antennas. (Only the passenger-side antenna is connected to the radio; the other antenna is a dummy.) Reflectors in the rear bumper mirror the taillights and suggest the circular taillamps that were associated with Fords for nearly a decade. Power assists include steering, brakes, and front seat.

The car's extra-cost 352-cid V-8 with four-barrel carburetor developed 300 bhp. It was mated to a Cruise-O-Matic three-speed automatic transmission. *Motor Trend* tested a Sunliner with this powerteam and achieved a 0–60-mph time of 11.7 seconds and a quarter-mile in 20.7 seconds at 80 mph.

Production of big Fords was down for 1960. The Starliner hardtop saw sales fall by 53,408 units compared to the 1959 Galaxie Victoria. The attractive convertible fared better and demand wasn't that far off from the previous year with 44,762 built versus 45,868 for the '59 Sunliner.

1960
Lincoln Continental Mark V Convertible Coupe

The same marketing philosophy that gave birth to the Edsel was also responsible for the slow-selling 1958–60 Lincolns. It's not that Ford Motor Company's planning committee was incompetent. Rather, the market changed drastically between the time when the Edsel and Lincoln were planned and when they arrived in showrooms for 1958. By then, the country had entered a sharp, although short-lived, recession. The downturn seemed to shake the public's "bigger is better" mind-set. Suddenly small and simple were in and excess was out.

The mood was different when the 1958-generation Lincoln was planned in 1955. The trim Lincolns that had dominated their class in Mexico's grueling Carrera Panamericana from 1952 to 1954 were always a distant second to Cadillac in sales. The 1956–57 Lincolns were bigger than the previous line and a better match for the luxury-class sales leader. For 1958, Lincoln leadership

decided that it would try to "out-Cadillac" Cadillac. The '58 was built on a 131-inch wheelbase—Lincoln's longest since the 1942 Custom formal cars. Plus, it was styled to look even more massive than its considerable 19-foot length. Although less ornate than other luxury cars, the new Lincoln was flamboyant with canted quad headlights.

The distinctive 1956–57 Continental Mark II hardtop coupe was a money loser, so the Continental name migrated back to Lincoln as the top trim level, distinguished by a unique reverse-slant retractable rear window—even on the convertible. The soft top also had a wonderfully complex folding mechanism with a powered metal panel that hid the top when folded. (The '58 Continentals were known as Mark IIIs, and by 1960 had advanced to Mark V.)

Earle MacPherson, Ford's chief engineer and inventor of MacPherson strut suspension, decided the new Lincoln would have unit-body construction—perhaps the biggest

unit-body car attempted at that time. The reinforcements necessary to achieve the structural rigidity expected of a Lincoln resulted in cars that could weigh more than 5000 pounds. FoMoCo established a plant in Wixom, Michigan, specifically for the production of unit-body cars, which also included the new four-passenger Ford Thunderbird.

Fortunately, Lincoln had a 430-cid V-8 with 375 bhp to provide excellent performance in spite of its heft. *Road & Track* recorded a 0–60-mph time of 8.7 seconds and a top speed of 115 mph. The price of performance was a 10-mpg thirst. Compression dropped for '59 and horsepow-

er slipped to 350. Then a switch from four- to two-barrel carburetion in pursuit of better fuel economy for 1960 saw output retreat again to 315 bhp. Surprisingly, the big Lincolns were nimble for their size and their handling drew praise from magazine road testers.

Despite good engineering, the big Lincolns didn't sell. Production dropped by 11,439 units for the 1958 recession year and continued to fall as other makes rebounded. Just 2044 of the facelifted $7056 Continental Mark V convertibles were made for 1960. It would take a smaller, classically styled car to restore Lincoln's fortunes in 1961.

1960
Rambler Six Custom Country Club Hardtop Sedan

After a rough start with the 1954 merger of Nash and Hudson and a brush with bankruptcy in '56, American Motors Corporation was financially secure by 1960. That year net sales exceeded the $1 billion mark for the first time and profits amounted to $48 million. The prime contributor was the midrange Rambler Six.

When Nash introduced a compact for 1950, it dug deep in the company's past to revive the Rambler name first used from 1902 through 1913. The renewed Rambler's wheelbase grew from 100 inches to 108 on newly introduced 1954 four-door models. With Nash and Hudson retired after 1957, all of AMC's subsequent products became some variety of Rambler: the 100-inch-wheelbase American, the 117-inch Ambassador, and the related Six and Rebel V-8 positioned between them on the 108-inch span.

AMC President George Romney was a zealous booster of compact cars but, until the 1958 recession, his pitch mostly fell on deaf ears. Then smaller, less ostentatious cars with good gas

mileage found greater favor. While sales of almost all American makes plummeted for '58, Rambler calendar-year retail sales more than doubled. American Motors was on a roll and made its first profit.

The Big Three brought out their own small cars for 1960. The American was smaller than the Chevrolet Corvair, Ford Falcon, and Chrysler Corporation's Valiant, but the Rambler Six was comparable in size to these new compacts. Rambler met them with a facelift. Tailfins were trimmed and windshield pillars shed their passé "dogleg." These and other changes helped keep Rambler in step with the times as styling moved from Fifties ornateness to the clean look of the Sixties.

Among the cleanest of the 1960 Rambler Sixes was the Custom Country Club hardtop sedan. Mysteriously, in the previous two years the upscale hardtop body style had only been available at the midline Super trim level. Then it moved to the top-line Custom series for 1960.

The Custom's standard-equipment comple-ment added an electric clock, upgraded interior trim, carpeting, thicker bodyside moldings, and full wheel covers. This car had a base price of $2458, but sold only 3937 units. The slow-sell-ing hardtop-sedan body style was dropped the next year and AMC never made another one.

Rambler's Nash and Hudson ancestors had been early pioneers of unibody construction and this was a selling point for Rambler. The Six's 195.6-cid engine also had Nash roots, dating back to the Nash 600 of 1941. Along the way, this powerplant gained displacement and was converted from side-valve to overhead-valve configuration for 1956. With a single-barrel car-buretor it developed 127 bhp, but put out 138 with an optional two-barrel carb. (A 200-bhp V-8 powered the Rebel that shared Six bodies, but in spite of fine performance, it didn't sell well.)

Big Three competition didn't slow Rambler down and Six sales rose by almost 55,000 units for 1960. Although there was trouble on the horizon, the early Sixties were good years for American Motors.

1961
Chevrolet Bel Air Two-Door Sedan

The finny 1959–60 Chevrolets were a response to Virgil Exner's exuberant '57 Chrysler Corporation styling, and they were bigger than the 1958 Chevys built upon what turned out to be a one-year-only body. The 1961 Chevrolets were a repudiation of the cars that immediately preceded them.

When it was time to come up with new designs for 1961, Bill Mitchell was head of General Motors Styling and the full-size Chevrolets had cleaner lines that would only get crisper as the decade progressed. Although the '61 Chevys

continued on a 119-inch wheelbase, the new bodies were shorter and narrower—yet were roomier inside. Doors were wider, seats were higher, and the trunk was larger. The decklid dropped to bumper height for easier loading.

A wide anodized-aluminum grille incorporated the headlamps, each within its own bezel. Turn signals tucked into the ends of a vented panel above the grille. A bold, uninterrupted crease that started at the leading edge of the hood dropped down the bodysides in a diagonal line, then turned up sharply near the back of the car, eventually forming an

overhang above the decklid and a deep "widow's peak" between the taillight groupings. The portion of the body above the crease line seemed to be draped over the lower portion like a cape. Rooflines contributed to light, airy looks. Pillared two- and four-door sedans had a shelflike roof with narrow C-pillars and a slight overhang above a large wraparound backlight, a look inspired by the dramatic 1959–60 GM four-door hardtops.

Three trim levels were offered: Impala and Biscayne at the top and bottom, respectively, with the Bel Air—reduced to being Chevy's midrange line since '59—in the middle. The brochure said "the Bel Air has all it takes to make it America's most popular model," though fancier and more expensive Impalas were Chevrolet's best sellers for '61.

To the bare minimum of amenities found in Biscaynes, the Bel Air sedans (and related Parkwood station wagons) added rear armrests, a cigarette lighter, a glove-box light, and automatic dome-light switches. Bel Airs also had additional trim inside and out. Back-up lights were optional and replaced two of the Bel Air's four taillights; only the Impala came with six taillights which included the back-up lights.

The chassis design with "X" frame and coil springs at each corner was retained. The frame was essentially a backbone chassis. Chevrolet strengthened the rocker panels, but many believed the car was vulnerable in side crashes. Still the frame provided good rigidity and the division bragged that the body had "725 insulating and cushioning points" to isolate passengers from vibration.

Chevrolet touted 24 power teams at the start of the year, and that increased with the midyear introduction of a high-performance 409-cid V-8 rated at 360 bhp. The entry-level engine was the 235.5-cid "Hi-Thrift" six that developed 135 bhp. A 283-cid "small-block" V-8 made 170 or 230 bhp, while the 348-cid "W-block" put out 250 to 350 bhp depending on carburetors and cam.

The base transmission was a three-speed manual. There was also a three-speed with overdrive and a four-speed stickshift. Available automatics were the popular two-speed Powerglide and—in its final year—the triple-turbine Turboglide.

A Bel Air two-door sedan with the six and three-speed was the least-expensive member of the series. It had a base price of $2384.

1961
DeSoto
Hardtop Coupe

The writing was on the wall for DeSoto in the late Fifties. Between the 1957 and 1958 model years, production plummeted from 117,514 to 49,445. In 1958, a bad year for almost every make, DeSoto fell harder than most. Later that year, DeSoto lost its dedicated factories; production moved to Chrysler's Detroit plant. Then, in late '59, the DeSoto Division was merged with Plymouth.

When Chrysler Corporation converted all its product lines except Imperial from conventional body-on-frame to unibody construction for the 1960 model year, it required a huge investment. Many experts didn't expect ailing DeSoto to make the jump, but Chrysler gave it another chance. However, the lineup was trimmed from four series on 126- and 122-inch wheelbases to two ranges on the 122-inch chassis. Station wagons and convertibles disappeared from the product mix. Canadian sales of the brand ended after the model year.

DeSoto returned to U.S. showrooms with a 1961 model, albeit briefly. The line was reduced to just one unnamed trim level, available in two- and four-door-hardtop body styles. The 1960 models shared new bodies with Chryslers, marked by pointed, canted tailfins. The 1961 touch-up for both included front-end styling with diagonally stacked headlights and a "chicken-wing" terminus for the fins that was stamped in the front-door sheetmetal. For brand differentiation, DeSoto received a controversial dual-element grille. A low, full-width grille sat between the

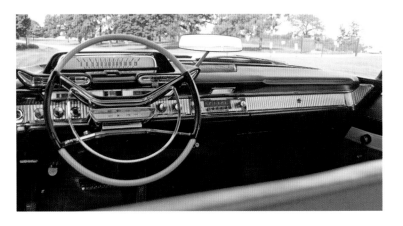

bumper and a projected upper vent upon which the brand name was spelled out in block letters. Inside, the DeSoto sported a revised instrument panel with a translucent speedometer.

Only one V-8 engine was carried over into '61, a 361-cid job that saw its compression ratio cut from 10.0:1 to 9.0:1 (the revised engine no longer required premium fuel) and output scaled back to 265 bhp. There were larger intake valves and an improved two-barrel carburetor. *Motor Trend* predicted, "Performance should be relatively unaffected." A new-design three-speed manual was the standard transmission, with the TorqueFlite automatic available at extra cost.

Chrysler Corporation's excellent torsion-bar front suspension and the more rigid unibody made Sixties DeSotos good road cars. *Motor Life*'s test of a 1960 Adventurer claimed, "On even the sharpest corners the Adventurer tracks true with no tendency for either end to break away from the circle. . . . On uneven roads practically the only vibration transmitted to the passengers is the audible slap of the tires against the pavement."

In spite of fine engineering and fresh styling, DeSoto demand fell to just 26,081 cars for 1960. Then, if going up against Ford and General Motors competition wasn't hard enough, for '61 DeSoto found itself being pressured by a new budget-series Chrysler, the Newport, on the same 122-inch wheelbase and with overlapping prices. Perhaps it's no wonder that DeSoto sales were utterly dismal. The '61s went on sale on October 14, 1960, and the last one of the 3034 built emerged on November 30, ending a marque history that dated to 1929. Just 911 were two-door hardtops that stickered for $3102 without options.

1962
Dodge Custom 880 Convertible Coupe

odge found itself in a jam for 1962. To a degree, Chrysler Corporation as a whole was wound up in the mess, which was a problem of its own making and would require some fast action and creativity to overcome.

In a major miscalculation, the standard '62 Plymouths and Dodges were downsized to almost midsized proportions. This left Chrysler a little thin on cars sized and priced to compete in the lower end of the medium-price field. DeSoto, which had occupied the space between Dodge and Chrysler, had been killed almost as soon as the 1961 model year began. The only reasonably priced big Mopar car was the Chrysler Newport.

Dodge dealers demanded a bigger car closer to what they were used to selling, and the corporation responded with blinding speed. Normally, Detroit took two to three years to develop a new car, but the Dodge Custom 880 was created in only three months. It was hardly a clean-sheet design, however: It was a '62 Newport with a slightly modified '61 Dodge Polara front end.

To further help a Chrysler pass for a Dodge, new corporate design head Elwood Engel applied some unique details including Dodge's new delta-shaped "fratzog" logo. (It's said that the logo's designer was told he had to name the emblem and came up with the nonsensical word.) The frat-

zog also appeared on the wheel cover's false knock-off hub. Inside was a Newport interior with a 1961 Polara dashboard and steering wheel.

Tooling up the Custom 880 cost only $400,00 and production commenced on January 22, 1962, with full production by February 2. Dodge had its new car fast and cheap.

The 880 rode on Newport's 122-inch wheelbase, a match for the previous year's Polara and much bigger than the 116-inch span of the '62 Dodge Dart and Polara. Like most Chrysler products from that year, there was rigid "Unibody" construction and torsion-bar front suspension.

To simplify the rush job, only one engine, a 361-cid V-8 shared with the Newport, was available. It had a two-barrel carburetor, 9.0:1 compression ratio, and put out a healthy

265 bhp. Dodge called the engine "high performance all the way," yet also claimed that it was economical and ran on regular gas. A three-speed manual transmission with floor shift was standard, but most buyers spent an additional $211 to get a three-speed TorqueFlite automatic with pushbutton controls. *Car Life* tested a TorqueFlite Custom 880 that accelerated from zero to 60 mph in 10.8 seconds and delivered fuel economy of 14–17 mpg.

Interiors were presented in a choice of cloth and vinyl or all vinyl in four colors, vinyl being standard on convertibles and station wagons. There were five body styles: four-door sedan, two-door hardtop, four-door hardtop, convertible, and hardtop wagon with six- or nine-passenger seating. Prices were the same or similar to comparable Chrysler Newports. The sales brochure made sure everyone knew that the Custom 880 was "THE 1962 DODGE FOR THE BIG CAR MAN!!"

The 17,505 cars sold for the short '62 model run (just 684 convertibles) helped some to alleviate a bleak year for Dodge dealers. The 880 grew to two trim levels in 1963, and—with a second facelift—continued on the same platform through 1964. By then some 77,531 had been built.

The 1962 Dodge Custom 880 convertible featured here is owned by Robert Price of Peoria, Illinois. The soft top originally cost $3251 and is one of only 684 built. This car sat for 30 years before it was restored to the condition seen here.

1962
Oldsmobile F-85
Jetfire Hardtop Coupe

G eneral Motors was flexing its engineering muscles in the early Sixties, especially when it came to the corporation's new Y-body small cars. The family of 112-inch-wheelbase premium compacts with unitized body construction included the Pontiac Tempest with independent swing-axle rear suspension, curved "rope drive" driveshaft, and a rear-mounted transaxle. Meanwhile, the Buick Special and Oldsmobile F-85 bowed in 1961 with an aluminum V-8, followed in '62 by a 90-degree V-6 initially exclusive to Buick.

As yet another example of Oldsmobile's history of pioneering engineering breakthroughs for GM products, in April 1962 the division introduced America's first mass-market turbocharged car, the F-85 Jetfire. (Chevrolet brought out its turbocharged Corvair Monza Spyder about a month later.) A turbocharger acts like a supercharger, albeit by

using the force of escaping exhaust gas to turn impellers that raise air pressure in the intake manifold, forcing the fuel mixture into the combustion chambers for more power. Working with Garrett AirResearch, Olds adapted a turbocharger to the 215-cid aluminum V-8. Where naturally aspirated versions of the engine made 155 or 185 bhp, the Jetfire's "Turbo-Rocket" version put out 215 bhp.

Turbo engines usually have reduced compression to avoid preignition or "pinging," but to reach the magic one-horsepower-per-cubic-inch mark, Olds engineers used a relatively high 10.25:1 compression. To head off detonation, an ingenious fluid-injection system added an equal mix of distilled water and methyl alcohol with a dash of rust inhibitor to the fuel mixture—they called it "Turbo-Rocket Fluid"—to lower the combustion-chamber temperature. A wastegate limited turbo boost.

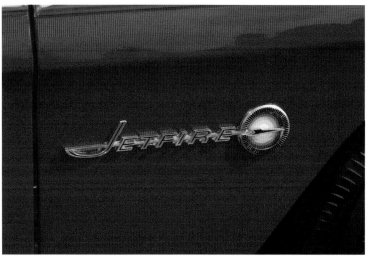

Inside, a vacuum-boost gauge on the standard center console indicated when the turbo was doing its job. The gauge also included a warning light to remind owners to refill the Turbo-Rocket Fluid tank—a bottle in the engine bay held an emergency supply.

A Jetfire could go from zero to 60 mph in 8.5 seconds and had a top speed of 107 mph. The quarter-mile run was achieved in 16.8 seconds.

All Jetfires were hardtop coupes, a new Y-body body style in 1962 with standard front bucket seats. Only 3765 were sold in the first year at a starting price of $3049, with a further 5842 built for 1963, the model's final year on the market. Approximately 50 of the '62s came with an optional four-speed manual transmission. (A "4S Hydra-Matic" was also available as an alternative to the standard three-speed stickshift.)

Oldsmobile tried a lot of ingenious engineering to make the turbo work, but ultimately the engine was unreliable in the hands of average owners who often failed to refill the Turbo-Rocket Fluid tank. In 1965, Olds recalled the Jetfires to swap the turbocharger for a conventional four-barrel carburetor. (It's estimated that only 30 to 35 with a functioning turbocharger remain.) Today, turbos benefit from computerized technology and are more popular because they increase power from small-displacement, fuel-efficient engines.

1962
Pontiac Bonneville Convertible Coupe

Back in 1962, Pontiac moved into the number-three sales position for the first time. The make's transformation from a frumpy old man's car to youthful performance machine was almost complete, and Pontiac would hold the third spot through the rest of the Sixties.

There were a lot of reasons for this run of success. The division offered a balanced array of boldly styled cars and available engines with lusty performance, particularly in the full-sized "standards." At the top of Pontiac's full-size-car hierarchy sat the Bonneville series.

The Bonneville got its start in 1957 as a limited-edition fuel-injected convertible within the Star Chief lineup, then stepped out on its own in '58 as a deluxe two-car series

with the addition of a low-roof hardtop coupe. The following year, Bonneville took on a four-door hardtop and a station wagon and replaced Star Chief as Pontiac's all-encompassing premium series.

Though Pontiac sales were led by the entry-level Catalina series as the division ramped up to its healthy market performance, it was in 1962 that model-year orders for Bonnevilles topped 100,000 for the first time. The $3570 convertible accounted for 21,582 of those cars.

Styling, which made good use of flowing "Coke-bottle" bodysides that flared in the rear quarters, was revised from '61 with a prominent upright "beak" dividing a grille of horizontal bars and a shift to C-shaped taillights. The two-door-

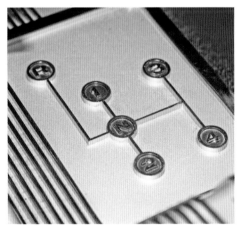

hardtop roof took on the fuller look of a raised convertible top. Most Bonnevilles rode on a 123-inch wheelbase and had an overall length of 218.6 inches, though the Custom Safari wagon was on a shorter 119-inch chassis.

Power was an important part of the picture, too. The vast majority of full-sized 1962 Pontiacs—save for those equipped with the rare Super Duty 421—had a 389-cid V-8 with horsepower ratings from 215 to 348. Most Bonnevilles were ordered with a Hydra-Matic transmission and had a 303-bhp engine. However, the extra-cost "Trophy 425A" engine shown developed 333 bhp, thanks to a special cam-shaft, stiffer valve springs, special exhaust manifolds, and 10.75:1 compression. It was joined to another desirable option, a four-speed manual transmission—a choice that

was becoming more popular for the early Sixties perfor-mance cars, but was still rare on full-sized luxury jobs. (Indeed, a mere 1909 Bonnevilles came from the factory with a three- or four-speed manual in '62.)

The sportiness factor was raised via options like leather-and-Morrokide vinyl bucket seats and Pontiac's exclusive "eight-lug" aluminum wheels. The latter consisted of a finned-aluminum brake drum at the center bolted to a steel rim. The wheels were functional as well as purposefully attractive. Aluminum dissipates heat better than iron, so the brakes were more fade resistant. Designed by Larry Shinoda, the wheels were built by Kelsey-Hayes and first appeared in 1960. When disc brakes began being more prevalent in the late Sixties, they were dropped after 1968.

1963
Chevrolet Corvette Sting Ray Coupe

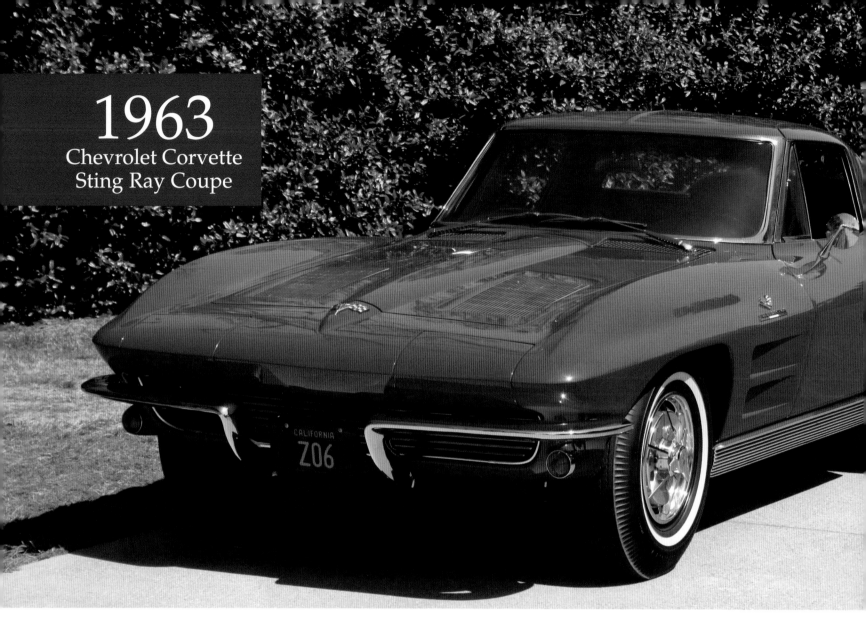

After 10 years on the market, the Chevrolet Corvette came out for 1963 as the most changed car in the history of the nameplate. Crisply creased styling of the fiberglass-bodied two-seater—"America's sports car"—borrowed liberally from a late-Fifties project known as the Q-Corvette, as well as the 1959–60 Stingray racer. Headlamps hid behind wedge-shaped doors that blended into the body above the low, full-width grille.

More significantly, for the first time there was a Corvette coupe. It featured a striking vertically-split rear window, as well as a roofline that tapered "boattail" fashion to a point on the deck. Priced at $4252, it cost $215 more than a Corvette convertible. The closed car drew 10,594 customers, but was slightly outsold by the ragtop.

Having picked up a second name, Sting Ray, this Corvette was new through and through, blending form and function in a more compact package. Two inches shorter and more than two inches lower than the '62 model, it

rode a 98-inch wheelbase that was four inches shorter than its predecessor. The new ladder frame served as an anchor for a sensational new independent rear suspension that improved ride and handling and reduced unsprung weight.

A 327-cid development of Chevy's "small-block" V-8 that was new for 1962 was continued. Four outputs were available from 250 to 360 bhp. The highest-powered version came with fuel injection and mechanical valve lifters. The "fuelie" mill could be had as a stand-alone option, but it was included with a Z06 performance-package option.

A three-speed manual transmission was standard. The Powerglide automatic was on offer, but 83.5 percent of 1963 'Vette enthusiasts spent $188 for a four-speed manual.

Zora Arkus-Duntov, the de facto chief engineer of the Corvette, hated the split-window "spine" that design vice president Bill Mitchell loved. Drivers didn't much care for it, either; it made backing up more difficult. Chevy obliged by making the '64 coupe's rear glass undivided, but history is fickle. Collectors now cotton to the original look and '63 coupes fetch a premium on the market.

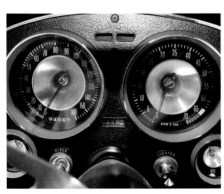

1963
Chrysler
Turbine Car

After jet turbines became the preferred propulsion for airplanes, it must have seemed natural that the piston engines in automobiles would also give way to turbines. (And according to popular magazines of the Fifties, cars would eventually fly.) The Big Three American automakers and Britain's Rover experimented with gas-turbine engines, but Chrysler, known for its advanced engineering, was clearly the most serious about them.

By the early Sixties, Chrysler had progressed to a fourth-generation automotive turbine and was ready to test the waters for mass production. Ghia, the Italian coach-builder that built Chrysler show cars, crafted 55 four-passenger hardtop coupes designed under the direction of Elwood Engel, recently recruited from Ford to head Chrysler styling—which explains the Turbine Car's resemblance to the period Ford Thunderbird. The Turbine Car didn't have the outlandish space-age styling of some concept cars. Yet its striking looks regularly turned heads and drew crowds on the street. Afterburnerlike back-up lights between the taillamps hinted at what was under the hood.

There were many hurdles to overcome before a jet engine would be practical in road traffic, and Chrysler had solved most. For instance, extreme exhaust temperatures were reduced by a "regenerator" that also improved fuel efficiency. The engine was smooth and sounded like a small jet—which was part of the car's allure.

The gen-four turbine was a compact engine that made 130 bhp and 425 pound-feet of torque, and was paired

with a TorqueFlite automatic minus the torque converter. Performance was comparable to that of a Chrysler Corporation 318-cid V-8. The turbine had a lag in throttle response and 0–60-mph acceleration exceeded 12 seconds. However, with the drag racing technique of building revs, then releasing the brakes, the car could run the quarter mile in an impressive low-13-second range. Top speed was close to 110 mph.

The gas turbine could burn all manner of fuels. Economy was all right on the open road, but bad around town. Part of the problem was that the engine idled at 18,000 rpm.

To test real-world durability and consumer reaction—and generate a boatload of publicity—203 average Americans (chosen from 30,000 requests) drove a Turbine Car for three months each. Forty-six cars were used during the two-plus years of the program, two Turbines were at the '64 World's Fair, two went on publicity tours, and five were prototypes. User feedback was positive, but the engines were costly to build, and tooling up for production was prohibitively expensive. Plus, looming emissions standards posed another problem. Chrysler never made a production turbine car, but experimented with the idea until 1981.

All but nine of the Turbine Cars were destroyed. Today, Chrysler retains two, two are in private collections, and five are in museums like the one seen here that is owned by the National Museum of Transportation in St. Louis. It is a rare museum Turbine Car that actually runs.

1964
Buick Riviera
Hardtop Coupe

It's puzzling that General Motors took as long as it did to respond to Ford's four-passenger 1958 Thunderbird. By the time GM introduced its own "personal-luxury" Buick Riviera for 1963, Ford had sold almost 350,000 T-Birds. Clearly Ford had found a highly profitable market niche. True, GM had the Pontiac Grand Prix, Oldsmobile Starfire, and Cadillac Eldorado before the Riv's debut, but these high-style machines based on existing models were a bit too big for the personal-luxury category.

It wasn't until late 1959 that GM began styling studies for what would become the Riviera. GM put its best talent on the job for what initially was planned as a LaSalle II for Cadillac—reviving the name of Cadillac's 1927–40 companion make. Bill Mitchell, head of styling at GM, decreed that the car would look like a lowered Rolls-Royce crossed with a Ferrari.

Ned Nickles, who had drawn up the '53 Buick Skylark and created Buick's signature "portholes," was in charge of the design. The result was a car with a crisp razor-edge

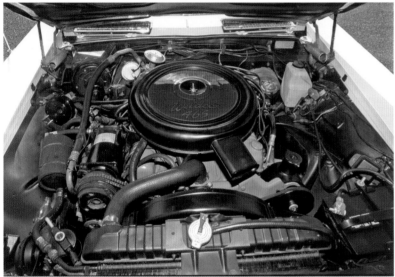

roof and elegant yet sporty lines. However, before it could arrive in showrooms, somebody had to agree to build it.

Cadillac was selling every car it could build and therefore wasn't interested. Instead, the LaSalle II project finally found a home at Buick. Buick had reached a sales peak in 1955 due mostly to its lower-priced Special line. Unfortunately, in order to build enough cars to reach the number-three sales position, quality had suffered. Additionally, the entry-level Specials had diluted the brand's premium image. Buick sales tumbled during the late Fifties. Things were turning around by the early Sixties, but management decided that an elegant personal-luxury car could do a lot to restore the brand's prestige. The Riviera name previously used for standard Buick hardtops was chosen for the new "halo" car. When it arrived, Italian designer Sergio Pininfarina described it as "one of the most beautiful American cars ever built."

While great pains had been taken with the Riviera's appearance, Buick was determined to get the engineering right as well. The Riv rode on a conventional Buick frame shortened to a 117-inch wheelbase—six to nine inches less than other Buicks. Care was lavished on the suspension to provide a luxury ride, all while delivering handling that lived up to the Riviera's sporty looks. Disc brakes weren't offered, but Buick's respected finned-aluminum front drums provided good stopping power.

Initially, a 401-cid, 325-bhp V-8 was standard with a 425-cid, 340-bhp V-8 optional. For '64, the 425-cube "Wildcat 465" (with a new automatic transmission) was standard and a 360-bhp "Super Wildcat" with dual four-barrel carburetors was optional. Performance was lively with 0–60-mph acceleration well under nine seconds.

Riviera was an instant hit. An initial production cap of 40,000 units was set, ostensibly to ensure an air of exclusivity. That target was met in the 1963 model year. Demand in '64 was almost as good, falling off to 37,658. Among year-two detail changes were the additions of a stand-up hood ornament, Riviera script on the decklid, and woodgrain trim on the center console.

The Riviera was the right car at the right time. The personal-luxury field filled out fast before the end of the Sixties, and would be red hot in the Seventies.

1964
Plymouth Sport Fury
Convertible Coupe

Immediately before big-engine/medium-body muscle cars became all the rage among hot-blooded drivers in the Sixties, there was a trend for mainline full-sized cars with lots of horsepower and deluxe trim inside and out. Following in the footsteps of the Chrysler 300s of the mid Fifties, most marques had a model in the same vein by early in the next decade.

Plymouth's liveliest family car was the Sport Fury. The nameplate first popped up in 1959, took a couple years off, then returned in 1962.

The revived Sport Fury package was a familiar one for its times, with a standard V-8 engine, sports-car-inspired interior with bucket seats and a center console, and body trim and wheel covers that were exclusive to the two-door hardtop and convertible that made up the series. But the '62s were the first of the downsized Plymouth standards hastily scaled down as a result of some erroneously interpreted information gleaned about rival Chevrolet's plans.

Sales suffered because the 116-inch-wheelbase Plymouths looked scrawny against their Chevy and Ford competitors—and they would have to stay on the platform until 1964. Along the way, there were attempts to make the cars at least look bigger, and exterior dimensions actually did increase slightly.

Nineteen sixty-four was the first year that Elwood Engel, Chrysler's head of styling since late '61, could have a major impact on the look of the corporation's cars. The cowl—and dashboard top—were flattened and front fenders and grille were pointed. In back, taillights became a little wider than they had been in '63. Sport Furys again followed the lead of the broader Fury series for body trim, but with red, white, and blue highlights. Sport Fury-specific wheel covers newly sprouted three-armed spinners from their centers.

As since '62, a 230-bhp 318-cid V-8 was standard in the Sport Fury. (Options in '64 ran up to a 426-cube "wedge-head" powerplant with as much as 425 bhp.) When the extra-cost TorqueFlite automatic transmission was ordered, the shifter was set in the console—replacing Chrysler Corporation's familiar dash-mounted, push-button shifting for the first time since 1956.

Model-year demand for Plymouths rose for a second straight year, moving the brand ahead of Oldsmobile into fourth place. The Sport Fury did its part: Orders jumped by almost 80 percent to 27,553, of which 3858 were the $3905 convertible. In 1965 there would once again be a Plymouth with the size and presence to ably compete with full-sized Chevrolets and Fords, and a Sport Fury convertible would serve as the pace car for the Indianapolis 500.

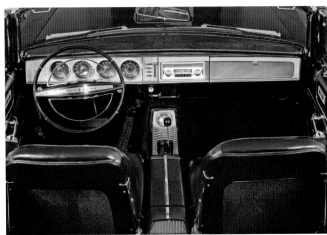

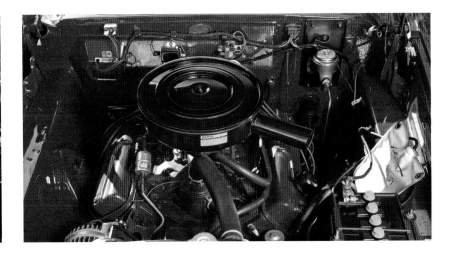

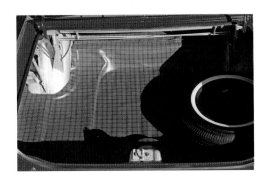

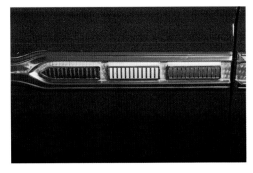

1964
Studebaker Daytona Convertible Coupe

tudebaker could perform miracles on a shoestring budget. It had to. By 1958 it was on the ropes and the end seemed near, but the South Bend, Indiana, company wasn't down yet. The 1959 Lark compact was created by reducing the wheelbase and trimming the overhangs of the full-sized Studebakers. Thus, this pruned Studebaker managed to be both compact outside and roomy inside.

Launched in a year when the only other domestic compact was Rambler's American, the Lark did wonders for Studebaker, pacing

a sales increase of more than 250 percent. Then, after the Big Three manufacturers entered the small-car field in '60, demand for Larks began slipping.

Industrial designer Brooks Stevens made the old Lark body look completely different for '64. He gave it crisper body contours, a fuller and more formal sedan/hardtop roof, and a horizontal grille that stretched to the headlight bezels. Meanwhile, Studebaker was phasing out the Lark name. (It persisted in print materials for some models.) In ascending order, series were the Challenger, Commander, Daytona, and Cruiser, with the sportiest body styles—the two-door hardtop and convertible—confined to the Daytona line. Wheelbase for all two-doors was 109 inches.

Engines for 1964 started with a 112-bhp, 169.6-cid six. Buyers had a wide choice of V-8s starting with a 259.2-cid job that put out 180 bhp with a two-barrel carburetor (shown here) or 195 horsepower with a four-barrel. A larger 289-cube V-8 developed 210 bhp with a two-barrel or 225 with four barrels. The Daytona hardtop was only available with a V-8; other Daytonas, including the convertible, could get the six as well.

There were also the "R" engines, high-performance V-8s developed by Andy Granatelli: a 289 that put out 240 (R1) or 290 (R2) bhp, the latter with a supercharger, and a 304.5-cid engine that produced 280 bhp with twin four-barrel carbs (R4) or 335 with supercharger (R3). Practically all 1964 Larks ordered with an "R" engine had one of the 289s—only one R3 car and a single R4 came from the factory.

Comfort and convenience options were plentiful and varied. For instance, the $2805 starting price of a V-8 Daytona convertible could balloon with the addition of things like an automatic transmission, power steering, and AM radio. Extra-cost curiosities included reclining front seats, a rarity on American cars in 1964, and front disc brakes, which weren't common in the U.S. until the late Sixties or early Seventies.

Studebaker built just 702 Daytona convertibles for the '64 model year. All told, it made 44,639 of the erstwhile Larks for the same period, a 40.8-percent decline from the year before, and another new low for the product line. A backdrop to all of this was the closure of the South Bend factory, which ceased vehicle production around Christmas 1963. All assembly shifted to Studebaker's more efficient Canadian plant in Hamilton, Ontario.

The closure of the South Bend facility put an immediate end to Studebaker's two personal-luxury models, the Thunderbird-like Gran Turismo Hawk and the dramatic fiberglass-bodied Avanti coupe, and its trucks. The '65 model year witnessed the absence of hardtops, convertibles, and Studebaker's own engines. The company's automaking operation was in a downward spiral and built its last car in March 1966.

1965
Mercury Comet Caliente
Convertible Coupe

Out of the product ferment bubbling up in the American auto industry in the Sixties, the intermediate class broached in 1962 by the Ford Fairlane and Mercury Meteor was on a high boil. In 1965, more than 2 million of the record 9.2-million-plus cars built for the model year were sized between the smallest compacts and the largest "standards."

Not all of those millions of "in-between" cars were true intermediates—not yet. A dwindling subset of the class were the so-called senior compacts, cars that had been designed to be a little bit bigger than the smallest models as befitted their attachment to brands from the medium-price segment. One of these was the Mercury Comet.

Launched in 1960 as an elongated and more-substantial-looking Ford Falcon, the Comet had, by mid-decade, come to hold a curious place at Mercury. It proved to be vastly more popular than the Meteor, and when the latter fell from the automotive firmament after just two years, the Comet effectively had to take its place.

The Comet had always been the largest of the senior compacts, and it became marginally wider and longer with

new sheetmetal for 1964, although the wheelbase was unchanged at 114 inches (save for station wagons, which shared Falcon's 109.5-inch span). Revised styling for '65, characterized by stacked headlights, made it bigger still. Inside was an attractive new dashboard with full instrumentation in round gauges.

Starting in '64 there were four trim levels: base 202, midline 404, luxury Caliente (Spanish for "hot"), and performance Cyclone. The lone convertible was found in the Caliente series. For '65, a 200-cid six with 120 bhp was made standard on all models except the Cyclone. A 289-cid V-8 developed 200 bhp with a two-barrel carburetor or 225 bhp with four-barrel and higher compression. The latter version was standard in the Cyclone and optional on other models, although Mercury dubbed all Comet V-8s "Cyclones."

The Caliente convertible cost $2664, but that was before any of the options found on this Ivy Gold example were added. In addition to the V-8 they include a three-speed Merc-O-Matic automatic transmission, rare AM/FM radio, wire-style wheel covers, back-up lights, interval windshield wipers, power steering and brakes, tinted glass, and an under-dash air conditioner. Many more were available.

Lincoln-Mercury Division went out of its way to promote Comet performance and durability. A team of '64 Comets was driven 100,000 miles in 40 days at Daytona International Speedway. Speeds averaged more than 105 mph. Nineteen sixty-five Mercury brochures still touted the Daytona feat, but a trio of that year's Caliente hardtops was subjected to a grueling 16,247-mile trip from the southern tip of South America to Fairbanks, Alaska.

In the '65 model year, when demand for Comets slipped by 13 percent to 165,052 cars, just 6035 convertibles were built. It's believed that only around 250 remain.

Comet's ambiguousness was definitively resolved for 1966. When the Fairlane was redone from the ground up, the small Merc joined it on the same intermediate platform.

1966
Chrysler 300
Hardtop Sedan

From 1955 through 1961, the number 300 meant one thing to Chrysler fans: brutal horsepower wrapped in a veneer of luxury. Those were the "letter-series" cars, identified by an annually advancing trip through the alphabet.

Then, in 1962, things changed. Now there were two cars by that, er, name—the 300-H in the "Beautiful Brute" tradition and a new, less-costly 300, the so-called Sport Series.

This latter 300 sans suffix was, in truth, a replacement for the Chrysler Windsor, priced between the entry-level Newport and premium New Yorker. It had most external trappings of the 300-H but with a less deluxe interior, tamer standard engine, and cushier ride. Both levels of 300s came as a two-door hardtop or convertible, but the Sport Series added a four-door hardtop.

Then, in 1966, things changed again. With the demise of the letter series following the 300-L of 1965, there was but one 300 again, the junior partner.

Even though it wasn't a letter car, the 300 Sport Series maintained an aggressive and sporty air relative to its fellow Chryslers. By '66 it was quite a different car, and in the

second year of an Elwood Engel-ordained design. As instituted for 1965, this wide "fill the box" look was enhanced by flat hoods and decklids. Bodysides alternately swelled and rolled between an upper "A" line trimmed with a bright molding and a lower skeg line. These simple, classic lines played well for the Chrysler Division, which sold almost 1 million cars during the 1965–68 design cycle.

Chrysler planners opted to lavish some extra money on the 300 for 1966. For the first time since '59, a 300 had a

distinct front end. Bumper and hood were V-shaped in plan view, which contrasted with the straighter lines of these parts found on Newports and New Yorkers. The grille design was specific to the 300 too.

The 300 was the only '66 Chrysler to employ taillights that wrapped around to the bodysides. The roof on the two-door hardtop folded around in back to frame a smaller rear window than that used by the brand's other coupes. Other series-exclusive identifiers included a stand-up hood ornament and two horizontal ribbed panels on each front fender that were long enough to extend into the doors.

To reinforce the notion that it was the sportiest of the Chryslers, the 300 came with front bucket seats—even in the four-door model. The '66 buckets were of a new shell style that boasted wider cushions, higher backs, and concealed "hockey-stick" hinges. Bright trim panels and color-keyed carpeting enhanced their rear surfaces. The standard armrest between the seats could be flipped up to allow a center passenger, but a new-style floor console was optionally available. Six all-vinyl, two cloth-and-vinyl, and two leather trims were listed. The well-equipped interior included a handy pull-out dashboard drawer that contained a coin sorter, storage compartment, twin ashtrays, and a cigarette lighter.

When it was go time, the 300 relied on a standard 383-cid V-8. Topped by a four-barrel carburetor, it produced 325 bhp. The power-hungrier could select a 375-horse-power 440-cube V-8—the TNT—as an option. A three-speed manual transmission was considered standard, with the popular TorqueFlite automatic on offer.

The 300 hardtop sedan weighed an even two tons, cost $3659, and drew 20,642 orders—8190 more than in 1965. It figured: After seeing production records in '65, Chrysler did better still in 1966—joint U.S./Canadian production hit 264,887.

1966
Chevrolet Impala
Station Wagon

O ne of the great things about Sixties American cars is that they could be ordered almost any way the customer desired. Some truly unique vehicles came down the lines. A fully optioned near-luxury car could have a three-on-the-tree manual transmission. A bare-bones base model might have factory air conditioning, while a Cadillac could be shipped without a heater.

That kind of freedom with the order sheet could also produce a highly desirable curiosity like a 1966 Chevrolet Impala station wagon that was half hauler and half hot rod. Selecting a high-performance "big-block" V-8, four-speed manual transmission, Positraction antislip rear axle, and metallic brake linings off the extensive Chevy options list stood to make one fast and capable "grocery getter."

Just a year after introducing the "Turbo-Jet" 396-cid engine, first of a new engine family for the division, Chevrolet went bigger in '66 with a 427-cube variant that got that way thanks to 0.16-inch-wider cylinder bores. The 427 was available in two versions. The fire-breathing L72 had mechanical valve lifters, big rectangular head ports,

high-rise aluminum intake, large-capacity four-barrel carburetor, and an 11:1 compression ratio. It was rated at 425 bhp. More suitable to conventional wagon duty—if such a thing can be said—was the L36 job that had hydraulic valve lifters, oval ports, and tamer 10.25:1 compression for 390 bhp. Both of the new engines generated a healthy 460 pound-feet of torque, albeit at different rpm.

A heavy-duty three-speed manual was the standard transmission with either 427. Alternatives to that were a three-speed Turbo Hydra-Matic automatic and a wide-ratio four-speed stickshift for the L36, or the choice of close- or wide-ratio "four on the floor" for the L72.

The 427s were available in any full-size Chevrolet model (and the Corvette). The division didn't break down engine and transmission installations by body style, so how many wagons had one of the 427s and a four-speed is unknown. However, 3287 of the 1,499,878 big cars made for '66 received the L36 and another 1856 ran with the L72.

Chevy "standards" had been redone from their new perimeter frame on up for 1965, so the '66s wore conservatively

modified sheetmetal as their chief difference. Lemonwood Yellow was one of 15 available paint colors. The station wagon family continued with Biscayne, Bel Air, and Impala models—and added one from the newly expanded "luxury" Caprice line, a car conspicuous by its faux-wood body trim.

Impala wagons came with a choice of six- or nine-passenger seating, the latter with a rear-facing third-row bench. In addition to its exotic powerteam, the example shown was originally built with options such as air conditioning with automatic climate control, cruise control, load-leveling rear suspension, tilt/telescopic steering wheel, AM/FM stereo, power windows, tinted glass, roof rack, and mag-style wheel covers. The 427 brought with it a tachometer that replaced the standard clock in the instrument cluster—but moved the clock to a pod atop the dash.

Rare options installed years later during the car's restoration were a 60/40 split-folding second-row seat and a carpeted load floor with stainless-steel trim. The latter was a Caprice wagon option that was extended to Impalas midyear. Also added was a rear sway bar.

1966
Plymouth Valiant Signet Hardtop Coupe

L ike all the domestic economy compacts that hit the American market in the early Sixties, the Plymouth Valiant soon added sportier hardtop and convertible models. Like all the compacts that eventually spawned racier "ponycars," the Valiant's bucket-seats-and-bright-trim jobs were quickly ignored.

The Valiant's splashiest version was the Signet, a name first applied to Plymouth's compact two-door hardtop in

1962. The next year brought a complete restyle to the Valiant with fuller lines and the addition of a pair of convertibles, one of them a Signet. The big news for '64 was a 273-cid V-8 option, but that was overshadowed by the springtime arrival of the Barracuda fastback. Aside from its big, sloping rear window, the Barracuda's visual and mechanical links to the Valiant were inescapable, and shoppers who wanted a racy small Plymouth flocked to it.

The Valiant would press on with further facelifts of the 1963-vintage body through 1966, maintaining the Signet hardtop and convertible along the way. Unchanged in all that time were Valiant's 106-inch wheelbase and Chrysler Corporation's de rigueur suspension set-up with front torsion bars and rear leaf springs.

For '66 styling still featured a single headlamp per side, but the lights were moved inside new straight-edged and forward-leaning front fenders. A newly flush three-element grille featured a body-color wedge in the center. Rear roof pillars were straightened up a bit; the rear window was enlarged; and the decklid, taillights, and bumpers were changed. Signets added a wide band of satin-silver "Aluma Plate" paint low on the bodysides.

Valiants adopted a new instrument cluster filled with rectilinear gauges. Signet interiors were clad in vinyl upholstery, but formerly standard bucket seats were now an extra-cost item, available in a choice of four colors.

For power, Valiants began with a 170-cid ohv "Slant Six" hooked to a three-speed manual transmission. That's what came for the $2261 starting price of a Signet hardtop—but digging a little deeper could procure a 145-bhp 225-cube six and TorqueFlite automatic transmission. When *Motor Trend* tested a 1966 hardtop with that powerteam, it went from zero to 60 mph in 13.6 seconds and turned in a 19.5-second quarter-mile. "The Plymouth Valiant Signet doesn't offer tire-smoking acceleration, but it does deliver decent performance for normal driving—and does it with an eye to economy," said *MT*, which noted 20-plus-mpg fuel mileage. The V-8, in two states of tune, remained available.

In '66 the Signet series accounted for 13,045 hardtops (down from a high of 37,736 for '64), plus another 2507 convertibles. An all-new sedan-only 1967 Valiant marked a return to the product line's workaday economy roots, while an expanded range of redesigned Barracudas catered to those who were looking for something on the sportier side.

1967
Chevrolet Camaro Rally Sport Convertible Coupe

When Chevrolet joined the "ponycar" club in 1967 it did a good job of making the all-new Camaro seem like it came in a wide choice of models. In addition to the basic hardtop coupe and convertible, there were high-performance SSes at the top of the lineup and stylish Rally Sports in between.

In truth, though, there really only were the basic models. It was option packages that transformed them into SSes or Rally Sports.

The "country-club Camaro" (as Chevy called it in one of the many magazine ads that ran for the new car), the Rally Sport was most notable for its blacked-out rectangle-pattern grille with headlights that could be hidden behind electrically operated doors. For a bit of flash, a wide, bright molding was added to the lower body between the wheel openings, which were highlighted with moldings of their own. Thin, color-keyed accent stripes ran along the fender-line. In back, black accents lined the inside surfaces of the deep taillight bezels. Hardtops were graced with bright drip moldings over the side windows.

The Rally Sport grille design required moving the parking/turn-signal lamps from inboard of the headlights to a place below the front bumper. Similarly, both back-up lamps were relocated from beside the taillight lenses to beneath the bumper. "RS" identifiers on the grille, front fenders, fuel-filler cap, and steering-wheel hub rounded out the package.

Rally Sport wasn't just the step up from the standard Camaro; it could also be paired with SS equipment (without the RS identification, however). For instance, the Camaro SS that served as the pace car for the 1967 Indianapolis 500 had the RS package.

While the SS laid sole claim to Camaro's use of 350-cid "small-block" and (from January 1967) 396-cube "big-block" V-8s, the base and Rally Sport cars both came in six-cylinder and V-8 subseries. A 230-cid, 140-bhp inline six and 327-cube, 210-horse V-8 were standard, respectively, with a 250-cid six of 155 horsepower and a 275-bhp 327 available at extra cost.

The standard transmission with sixes and 327s was a three-speed manual, synchronized in all forward gears, with column shift. A floor-shift four-speed and Powerglide two-

speed automatic with column or floor shift were available at extra cost. Final drive with most sixes and 327s was 3.08:1, but Powerglide cars without air conditioning got 2.73:1 cogs—unless they were Rally Sports, which retained the more aggressive ratio.

Chevy's first Ford Mustang-fighter sat on a 108.1-inch wheelbase. A preview of the next-generation Nova due for '68, it had unitized body construction with a separate front subframe to cradle the engine and hold the coil-and-wishbone suspension. The conventional solid rear axle was supported by novel single-leaf semielliptical springs. Drum brakes were standard, with front discs optionally available.

This Nantucket Blue example is one of the 19,856 V-8 convertibles built out of 25,141 total 1967 Camaro ragtops. With a two-barrel carburetor and 8.75:1 compression ratio, its engine made 210 bhp at 4600 rpm and 320 pound-feet of torque at 2400 rpm. An open V-8 Camaro like this started at $2809 in 1967, but it didn't finish there when accumulating add-ons like the Rally Sport package ($105.35), Powerglide ($194.85), power steering ($84.30), a tinted windshield ($21.10), rear bumper guards ($9.50), wheel covers ($21.10), whitewall 7.35×14 tires ($52), and a pushbutton AM radio ($57.40).

1967
Plymouth Fury III Hardtop Coupe

Plymouth got off to a rocky start in the Sixties. First, unusual styling for 1960 and '61 failed to find favor in the marketplace. Then, 1962–64 models that were hastily shrunk to cover a shortened 116-inch wheelbase left Plymouth smaller than its Ford and Chevrolet competition in an era when bigger meant better to many car buyers. Sales slipped further.

In the interim, Elwood Engel, ex of Ford Motor Company, replaced Virgil Exner as vice president of styling at Chrysler Corporation, and his more "commercial" approach for the facelifted '64 Plymouths began to turn things around for the brand. Then, the company committed to a new family of 1965 C-body full-sized Plymouths, Dodges, and Chryslers.

Plymouth switched to a 119.5-inch wheelbase (121.5 for wagons) that effectively matched its Ford and Chevy rivals. The styling was mainstream and linear, yet clean and elegant. Model-year production for the full-sized Plymouth jumped to 329,950 units—a big improvement from 1962's low of 182,520 "standards."

Still, Plymouth was fourth in sales. Even bolstered by sales of compact and midsize cars, the brand couldn't reclaim its traditional third place, now tenaciously held by Pontiac. At least it was sustaining itself by the mid Sixties. Demand for the big Plymouth dropped a little to 318,431 for '66 and then ever so slightly again to 317,310 for 1967 when the car had revised styling.

The stacked-headlight alignment of 1965–66 was continued, but the fender tops above them were canted down towards the hood instead of flat as before. Bodysides adopted a kickup in the rear-quarter panels, another loosening of the strict lines that defined the previous models. Taillights—in clusters of two or three per side, depending on the trim level—rested in a sunken cove between the bumper and the trunklid, which sprouted a kind of beak at its center. Sedan and hardtop rooflines were completely redone; a second "Fast Top" hardtop-coupe roof with bell-bottom triangular sail panels was added for higher-end trim levels.

Although Plymouth might have made some miscalculations about size and styling in the Sixties, the engineering was always excellent. Stiff unibody construction and the highly regarded corporate torsion-bar front suspension provided good large-car ride and handling.

Engine choices for 1967 ranged from the thrifty and durable 145-bhp Slant Six to a powerful 375-bhp 440-cid V-8. The base V-8 still displaced 318 cubic inches and put out 230 bhp, but it was of a new "LA" series that was lighter and used wedge- instead of poly-spheric-shaped combustion chambers. A three-speed manual transmission was standard, with a four-speed manual and three-speed TorqueFlite automatic available.

The model range included the Fury I, Fury II, and Fury III; a plush VIP that was a response to Chevrolet's top-line Caprice and Ford's LTD; and the Sport Fury for those who preferred the sporty ambience of a hardtop coupe or convertible with bucket seats and a center console. Fury III was the well-rounded, high-volume series that direct-ly contended with the industry heavyweights Chevrolet Impala and Ford Galaxie 500. A two-door hardtop with the base V-8 (shown) started at $2872, but typical for the times it required more to equip one with features like power steering and brakes, automatic trans, a convenience light package, sport wheel covers, and a vinyl top.

1967
Rambler Rebel SST Hardtop Coupe

The Rambler Rebel, American Motors's entry in the still-expanding intermediate segment, was all new for 1967. It was larger than the car it replaced, took on a changed driveline and rear suspension, and welcomed a more powerful V-8 to the top of its engine roster.

Even the name reflected a change. What had formerly been known as the Classic series was now dubbed Rebel, a moniker Rambler first used from 1957 to 1960 on V-8-powered compacts and recently revived for a specially trimmed '66 Classic hardtop. This new full family of Rebels ascended in three trim levels from 550 to 770 before finally peaking at SST—which was restricted to a two-door hardtop and convertible.

The Rebel shared a new unibody structure with the full-size Ambassador. The Rebel ran a 114-inch wheelbase, up two inches from the '66 Classic, which was truly one of the last senior compacts. (The '67 Ambassador sat atop a 118-inch span.) In addition, the handsome new body was four inches wider than the previous shell, ensuring generous interior room. The cars were longer, too.

With a decent budget in hand, AMC stylists came up with an exterior design that clearly broke with the past. This was especially true in the curvier, more fluid bodysides and the attractive cantilever roof for two-door cars.

Underneath was a new rear suspension. Coil springs were retained, but they now supported a four-link setup.

Also, the old torque tube was replaced with an open drive-shaft. The overall effects were a smoother ride and stability and handling improvements that didn't go unnoticed in the automotive press.

There was also news under the hood, where the top option was a new 343-cid V-8 that developed 235 bhp with a two-barrel carburetor or 280 with a four-barrel and a higher 10.2:1 compression ratio. The latter was the only engine on the Rebel roster that required premium gas.

The other engines were also relatively fresh. The 200-bhp, 290-cid V-8 was just one year old. Both V-8s were labeled "Typhoon" and AMC claimed they had "the lightest 'reciprocating mass' in the industry. Translation: A Typhoon's rods, pistons, and the like weigh less than anybody's." Low reciprocating mass meant greater efficiency and throttle response.

The base "Torque Command Six" dated to 1964, and variations of it would power various AMCs and Jeeps as late as 2006. A modern ohv powerplant with seven main bearings and a thin-wall block, it delivered a good balance of performance and economy. The 232-cid six made 145 bhp with a single-throat carb or 155 bhp with a two-barrel.

SSTs cost $2872 as a convertible or $2604 as a hardtop. The closed car came standard with reclining front bucket seats clad in "Cherbourg" fabric and vinyl, and a unique pair of throw pillows in matching cloth were available at extra cost. Standard full wheel covers could be swapped for optional turbinelike "Turbo-Cast" wheel covers.

A redesigned model with so much going for it should have sold well, but Rebel sales actually declined 20 percent from the Classic's 1966 totals. As the Rambler brand name was being phased out, the Rebel formally became an AMC model for '68, but sales continued to slide. The Rebel was replaced by the Matador for 1971.

1968
Dodge Dart GTS
Convertible Coupe

During the Sixties, the automobile market fractured into several different segments within the industry's overall scope. To be successful, most makes could no longer rely on a single one-size-fits-all strategy.

Detroit's Big Three added their first compacts for 1960. Midsize—or intermediate models—arrived on the market by 1962. The "ponycar" craze started with the introduction of the Ford Mustang and, to a lesser degree, the Plymouth Barracuda, both in April 1964.

Then, too, muscular performance variants of full-size cars and sporty compacts also appeared early in the same decade. Soon these categories started cross-pollinating, and within a few years a bevy of new models to fill an array of new niches appeared.

At Dodge, the Dart name appeared in more market segments than most during the Sixties. As introduced for 1960, Darts were full-sized cars. By 1962, due to the downsizing of Dodge's full-size products, Darts were in effect intermediates. The next year, the nameplate shifted to the division's redesigned entry in the incredibly competitive compact class, the car that was previously known as the Lancer.

A sporty Dart GT model with bucket seats had been part of the mix since '63, but things became substantially more interesting the next year when Chrysler's new 273-cid V-8 joined the options list. Though a huge improvement, the first V-8 available in a Dodge compact wasn't a complete screamer with only 180 bhp on tap.

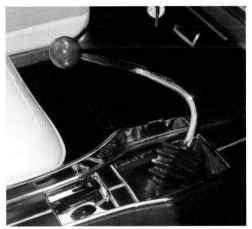

A 1967 redesign left Dart looking better than ever. Lacking a ponycar like the Barracuda, it still offered convertibles and hardtops. The GT remained the performance model and, at first, the 273 ruled the roost. But very late in the year, Dodge released a new top-performance Dart: GTS, with a 280-bhp 383-cid V-8 and meatier suspension.

As interesting as this development was, the picture changed a bit for 1968. Like all '68 Darts, the GTS (or GTSport as the catalog copywriters called the brute), wore the expected facelift. But GTS models also received some unique visual touches including a distinct power-bulge hood. Bold "bumble-bee" stripes that wrapped around the rear quarter panels and across the top of the decklid were available to GTS buyers. The striping scheme clearly signaled to those in the know that your Dart was a member of Dodge's "Scat Pack" of hot performers.

Underhood there were major changes. The 383 was back and raised to 300 bhp, but now it was optional. The standard mill was a new 340-cid version of the 273 V-8. The high-performance 340 was a thoroughly modern design, compact and lightweight—qualities the 383 lacked. A four-speed manual or TorqueFlite were transmission choices.

Rated conservatively at 275 bhp—many believed the true number was closer to 325—the 340 was a stormer in the Dart. *Car and Driver* reported that its tested 340 GTS went from zero to 60 mph in six seconds flat and covered the quarter in 14.4 clicks at 99 mph. This was better than a 375-horse Chevy II or 383-powered Plymouth Road Runner.

After its start as a rare GT option package in 1967, the GTS became a full trim level for '68, when Dodge sold 8745 of them, including just 450 convertibles. Demand slacked off to 6702 in 1969, the last year for the GTS.

1968
Ford Mustang High Country Special Hardtop Coupe

One of the first special editions of the iconic Ford Mustang was the High Country Special. In 1966, perhaps to maintain sales momentum in the car's second model year, Denver-area Ford dealers offered a High Country Special with unique paint colors and brass badges for the front fenders. Available in all three Mustang body styles, 333 were sold for '66 and another 416 moved off the lots in 1967.

A more distinctive High Country Special arrived during 1968 with assists from Carroll Shelby and California. Shelby built a prototype notchback hardtop coupe known as "Little Red." Although the car didn't enter production as one of the souped-up Mustangs the ex-champion sports car racer was turning into Shelby GTs, it did get the attention of Ford Southern California District Sales Manager Lee Grey. He lobbied for a Little Red-flavored special.

The resulting Mustang California Special didn't have the supercharged 427-cid V-8 or other mechanical perks that Shelby gave to Little Red, but it got some of the styling touches. Added to the hardtop coupe were a rear spoiler that wrapped around the rear fenders, multisection taillights from the 1965 Thunderbird (albeit without the sequential turn signals), pop-off gas cap, unique bodyside scoops, special stripes, hood locks, Mustang GT-style hubcaps, and a blacked-out grille sans the Mustang emblem but with free-standing fog lights. (Hood vents with integrat-

ed turn signals were standard on all '68 Mustangs.)

The High Country Special was the California Special, sans California Special script on the rear fenders. Also, "GT/CS" graphics on the side scoops were replaced by a High Country Special shield that featured a horse galloping above mountain peaks.

The Specials could be ordered with any available Mustang powertrain. New for the year was a 230-bhp 302-cid V-8,

the latest development of Ford's family of thin-wall "small-block" engines.

Mustangs were a common sight in 1968, so the opportunity to get what appeared to be a Shelby-like customized Mustang at a reasonable price must have been appealing. All High Country Specials were made in Ford's San Jose, California, plant, which built 4118 units, 251 as High Countrys—and only one of which was equipped with a center console.

1968
Lincoln Continental
Four-Door Sedan

Continental

Lincoln rebooted its styling themes several times in the Fifties, but couldn't dent Cadillac's postwar dominance of the luxury market. In fact, in 1958, Ford Motor Company Vice President Robert McNamara was on the verge of recommending that Lincoln be retired, unhappy as he was with that year's all-new but unpopular (and unprofitable) Lincolns and Continentals.

Meanwhile, other FoMoCo executives equally cognizant of Lincoln's struggles concluded that the lack of design consistency was hurting the brand. They determined that stretching the design cycle to as long as nine years would help establish a Lincoln "look," reduce body-tooling costs, and raise resale values—which would be a lure to buyers.

McNamara was persuaded to give Lincoln another chance in its next scheduled full redesign, due for 1961, with the caveats that the next design be reasonably sized and profitably built. A short (by luxury-car standards) 123-inch wheelbase was selected and an elegant, slab-sided design directed by Elwood Engel was chosen. Only two body styles were produced, a thin-pillar four-door sedan and a four-door convertible, both with rear-hinged "suicide doors" in back that made exits from the back seat easier.

The classically simple 1961 Lincoln Continental lacked faddish design clichés, so its look aged well. Plus, sales were increasingly better—though still no threat to Cadillac. There were annual appearance tweaks and a wheelbase stretch to 126 inches in '64, but a more thorough facelift was deemed necessary by 1966. This updated version of the successful 1961 design was subtly different—a little sharper-edged—but still imparted the tasteful spirit of the

original. Also, a two-door hardtop joined the line. With yearly detail tweaks, this form continued through 1969.

The push for a sustainable styling identity was matched by a heightened emphasis on construction quality. Lincoln claimed that it took four days to build a car, the first two of which were devoted to assembling the unitized body. The finished products were subjected to a 90-minute inspection, including a 12-mile road test, before being approved for delivery.

For 1968—the year in which the 1-millionth Lincoln was built—the Continental was updated with a new grille surface organized in six groups of six flat, wide rectangles. At the ends of the grille were wraparound parking lights that tucked into the upright fender ends. In a similar fashion, for the first time since 1965, taillight lenses were

notched into the rear fenders above the bumper ends. Both satisfied new federal requirements for side-marker lights.

The convertible was dropped after 1967, so that left a product mix of the sedan, hardtop, and factory-authorized and warranteed long-wheelbase Executive Limousine conversions. The hardtop sported a new more "formal" roofline with wider sail panels. Early '68s had the 462-cid V-8 with 340 bhp that came in with the 1966 model. As a running change, this was replaced by a 460-cube V-8 that was engineered to run cleaner. It made 365 bhp and an impressive 500 pound-feet of torque.

Continental assemblies dipped to 39,134 for model-year 1968, including 29,719 sedans. But with 7770 of the new Continental Mark III personal-luxury hardtop coupes added in, overall Lincoln production slightly bested the '67 total.

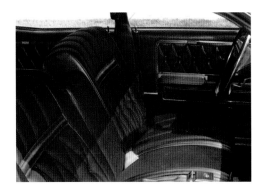

1969
AMC Javelin SST
Hardtop Coupe

After its successes of the late Fifties and early Sixties under the direction of George Romney, American Motors Corporation stumbled in the mid Sixties under his successor, Roy Abernethy. One misstep was the firm's first attempt to create a small, sporty car which might appeal to the "youth market" that U.S. automakers saw arising.

The fastback Tarpon show car of 1964 was based on the freshly redesigned platform of the compact Rambler American. Had AMC stayed with the well-received original concept, it could have had an ideal match to compete with the Ford Mustang and Plymouth Barracuda in 1965. Instead,

the fastback—now called Marlin—was stretched to fit on the next-size-up Classic chassis. The Tarpon's impish aura was lost. Sales were sluggish—and became only more so through 1967, when Marlin was incongruously shifted to the large Ambassador platform.

However, even as the Marlin was beginning its doomed march through the marketplace, a replacement was already in the works—the Javelin, which made its debut for 1968. Set on a 109-inch wheelbase, it was a proper "ponycar" in a class that already included the Mustang, Barracuda, Chevrolet Camaro, Pontiac Firebird, and Mercury Cougar.

Richard Teague's styling staff produced a long-hood/short-deck design with semifastback styling that drew praise. Relative to other ponies, the Javelin came with a little extra interior room than most and prices that tended to undercut the competition.

There were base and tonier SST versions. The SST included reclining front seats—unusual in American cars at the time—a sport steering wheel, woodgrain interior trim, and wide rally stripes. Engines ranged from a 145-bhp six to a 280-bhp, 343-cid V-8. A dual-exhaust 390-cid V-8 that developed 315 bhp became optional midyear. To the standard coil-and-wishbone front suspension and parallel-leaf rear suspension buyers could add a handling package with a front sway bar and heavy-duty springs and shock absorbers.

Reviewers had good things to say about Javelin's performance and handling. The car went racing and competed against other ponycars in the Sports Car Club of America's Trans-Am series. AMC hoped to sell 35,000 to 40,000 units, but instead moved 56,462 Javelins for the '68 model year. Not only did the car sell well, but it brought younger customers into AMC showrooms. The company was on a roll and turned a profit.

Javelin had few changes for its second year, when demand cooled a bit to 40,675 cars. A new surface to the divided grille now sported a small red, white, and blue roundel on the left side. Javelin call-outs were moved to the hood and roof sail panels. Starting in January '69, the cars could be ordered in one of three bold "Big Bad" colors, which included color-matched bumpers.

The 390 V-8 could be paired with a four-speed manual gearbox or automatic transmission. SSTs with the 390 were eligible for a Go Package option that included power front disc brakes, the handling package, redline tires on styled-steel wheels, and nonfunctional hood scoops. Some other available extra-cost items were a tachometer, 140-mph speedometer, bodyside rally stripes, and a vinyl roof covering.

1969
Chevrolet Chevelle
Malibu Hardtop Coupe

Not too big. Not too small. That succinctly sums up the class of midsized cars that sprang up early in the Sixties and increasingly appealed to American consumers as the decade played out.

In that time, only four major brands declined to enter the segment, and they were luxury or near-luxury marques that didn't (yet) see smaller cars fitting their image. Some of the entries in the intermediate field had bulked up from their original configurations as "senior compacts" after Ford hit pay dirt with the 115.5-inch-wheelbase Fairlane that bowed in 1962. While appealing to budget-conscious consumers of family cars (to many, the intermediates were about the same convenient size as mid-Fifties Fords, Chevrolets, and Plymouths), the midsizers also made a play for the "youth market" because they were just big enough to hold the biggest V-8s of the day. This gave rise to the artfully packaged muscle cars that became a significant market niche of the late Sixties.

Model-year 1969 saw the intermediates account for 25.9 percent of the 8,821,599 U.S. cars manufactured to '69 specifications. As it had been in most years since the late Twenties, Chevrolet was the top overall producer. Perhaps it's no surprise, then, that it was home to the most popular of the midsizers, the Chevelle.

The Chevelle had been around since 1964. When General Motors grew the Pontiac Tempest, Oldsmobile F-85, and Buick Special to fit a new corporate "A" body on a 115-inch wheelbase, making them true intermediates, Chevy was invited to join the party. A drastic A-body redesign for 1968 came with a two-tiered chassis program: Four-door cars and most wagons were on a 116-inch wheelbase; two-doors rode a 112-inch span that gave coupes and convertibles better proportions and sportier looks.

A-body appearance changes for '69 were limited. All two-door hardtops and convertibles shed their side-window vent wings. Chevelles' revised grille featured a horizontal center bar and larger taillights that no longer wrapped around the rear quarters.

The runaway popularity leader of the Chevelle clan was the nicely outfitted Malibu series, and the clear favorite

of Malibu buyers was a hardtop coupe like the one seen here in Frost Lime and Cortez Silver with a Midnight Green vinyl top. Seats in the Medium Green interior are completely trimmed in vinyl, which was an option—cloth-and-vinyl upholstery was standard in two- and four-door hardtops and the four-door sedan.

It took $2726 to secure a Malibu hardtop coupe with the base V-8, which displaced 307 cubic inches. The 307 bowed in '68 as a replacement for the venerable 283, its extra cubes coming from a 0.25-inch-longer stroke. Topped with a two-barrel carburetor, the 307 was factory rated at 200 bhp (though changes made to this car include the additions of a dual-exhaust system and a four-barrel carb not native to the 307). A two-speed Powerglide automatic could be ordered in place of the standard three-speed manual gearbox.

1970

Dodge Coronet Super Bee Hardtop Coupe

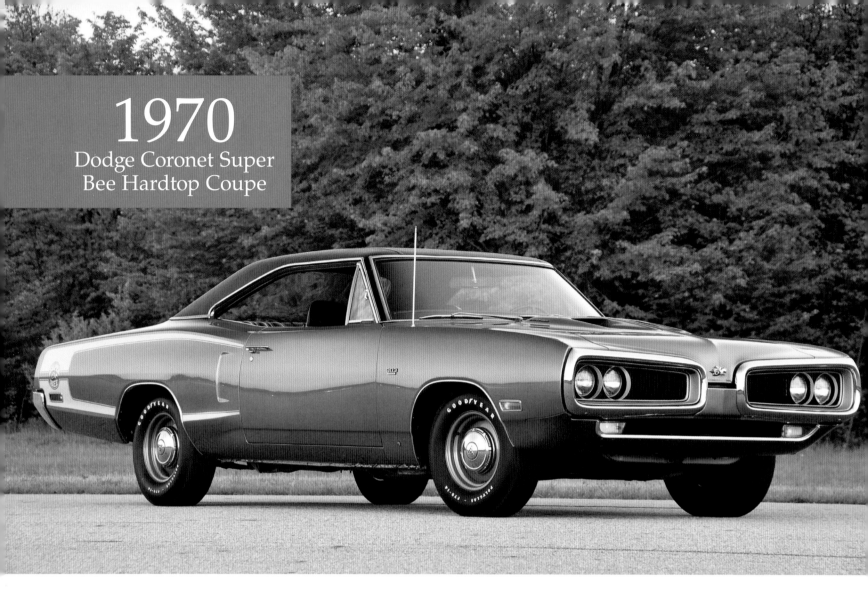

The midsize muscle car was the apple of the eyes of those who filled Detroit's coveted youth market in the Sixties. There was just one problem: That wasn't exactly the wealthiest segment of society. The Pontiac GTO and the crop of direct imitators that sprang up right behind it followed a formula. This included high-powered engines and other driveline and chassis enhancements, of course, but also packed on costly "sports car" features that dazzled young-thinking buyers—bucket seats, fancy trim, exterior scoops and stripes, custom wheel treatments, and more. As such, a fully equipped and well-optioned boulevard blaster could be out of reach for many of the drivers most likely to want one.

Enter the 1968 Plymouth Road Runner. It used the same intermediate platform as the flashier GTX, but it eschewed plush frills—and some standard horsepower—to pare the purchase cost, allowing customers to put their remaining resources toward go-fast options. Popular from the start, it proved that a car with a hot engine but no excess of luxuries could be a big seller.

The Coronet Super Bee was Dodge's version of the Road Runner. In name, it sprang from a Coronet convertible customized to serve as an attraction for the 1968 Detroit Auto Show, where it was well received. A production model was announced that February. Introduced as a pillared coupe with a hinged rear-quarter window, it was joined by a hardtop with fully retractable side glass in '69. (Ironically, considering its show-car ancestor, the Super Bee never came as a convertible like the Road Runner.) For 1970 it shared the most striking feature of the Coronet facelift, a loop-style front bumper rendered as a double delta.

Road Runner's Saturday-morning-cartoons mascot was mirrored in the Super Bee by the supercharged honeybee that served as the emblem of Dodge's "Scat Pack" collection of high-performance autos. The standard engine in both was a 383-cid V-8 with a four-barrel carburetor and high-lift camshaft that put out 335 bhp. The Super Bee was capable of accelerating from 0 to 60 mph in about seven seconds, and ran the quarter mile in around 15 seconds.

Super Bee buyers with some extra cash to spend could get more power if they preferred. The celebrated 426-cube

dual-quad Hemi with 425 bhp was available throughout the car's run, and 1969 saw the debut of the 440 Six Pack, a 440-cid mill that made 390 ponies with triple two-barrel carbs atop a high-rise aluminum Edelbrock intake manifold.

A four-speed manual was standard in 1968 and '69. In 1970, the four-speed—now with a pistol-grip shifter—joined the TorqueFlite automatic on the options list as a floor-shift three-speed became standard. Features of the 117-inch-wheelbase chassis included torsion bars, rear leaf springs, shock absorbers, and 11-inch drum brakes that were all rated heavy duty. A 150-mph speedometer and full gauge package came standard—but a tachometer cost extra.

Super Bees sprang from two-door models of the demure Coronet 440 line. A bench front seat was standard but buckets were available. The 1970 hardtop coupe started at $3074, or $495 less than a showier Coronet R/T hardtop. The Super Bee hive consisted of 15,506 members in '70.

1970
Mercury Cyclone
Hardtop Coupe

Nineteen seventy has come to be considered the peak of the muscle car era. Driven from behind by an escalating horsepower race that continually pushed up outputs, but hemmed in ahead by looming federal regulations that would be met by tamer engines able to run on cleaner-burning fuels, things would never be better for the power-hungry motorists of the era.

The classic midsize muscle car knew almost no bounds of price or class. All but one marque in the low- and medium-priced classes offered one sooner or later. The more upscale brands brought out their interpretations with better-trimmed interiors and additional standard equipment. Ride and sound insulation of the tonier ones also tended to be better than on cheaper, higher-volume models.

A good example of one of these gentleman's muscle cars was the Mercury Cyclone. It was the sport version of the intermediate Montego product line, which itself was an upmarket companion to the Ford Fairlane/Torino.

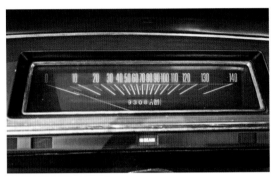

Mercury's performance image got a boost from NASCAR victories in the late Sixties and early Seventies. The 1968 Cyclone used the same basic body shell as the Fairlane, but the Merc was a mile or two per hour faster thanks to the better aerodynamics of the Mercury grille—and the advantage over Plymouth and Dodge rivals was even greater. Although Cyclones shared showrooms with big, plush Park Lanes and Marquis, racing success made shopping for a performance car in a Mercury store seem less odd.

For 1970, Cyclone had new styling that swapped a fastback roofline for a less-aerodynamic semifastback. Still, Mercurys continued to score track victories. The Cyclone's most distinctive appearance feature was a thrusting grille with a protruding "gunsight" centerpiece.

All Cyclones had unibody construction and a 117-inch wheelbase. Engine choices ranged widely, from a 250-bhp 351-cid V-8 to a Super CJ 429-cid V-8 underrated at 375 bhp. Front disc brakes provided good stopping power for a nearly two-ton car with powerful V-8 engines.

Cyclones came in three levels: base, sportier GT, and high-performance Spoiler. The base Cyclone was akin to the Plymouth Road Runner in that it had a standard bench seat and limited amenities, but concentrated on performance with a high-output engine and four-speed transmission with Hurst shifter. Still, at $3228 to start, it cost a good $500 less than a Spoiler.

The Cyclone's standard 360-bhp 429 V-8 was an option for the costlier Cyclone GT that had more show but less go with its 250-horse 351. The buyer of a base Cyclone could dress it up with bucket seats, a special instrument package (tachometer, oil pressure, temperature, and ammeter gauges), Select-Shift automatic transmission, AM radio, air conditioning, tinted glass, and power steering and brakes. Not optional on the base Cyclone—but possibly available from dealers—were styled wheels, a decklid spoiler, and body stripes similar to those found on the Cyclone Spoiler.

To publicize the performance potential of the redesigned 1970 Barracuda, Plymouth went racing. The Sports Car Club of America's (SCCA) Trans-Am series was where "ponycars" proved their mettle. Mustang and Camaro had been dominating the series, but Plymouth hoped to muscle its way in.

Barracudas were built in three series: base, luxurious Gran Coupe, and 'Cuda. The last picked up on car-buff slang for the Barracuda; Plymouth made it official as the handle for the highest-performance series. Naturally, the 'Cuda was chosen for SCCA duty.

Plymouth turned to racing legend Dan Gurney and his All-American Racers (AAR) team to manage the factory-sponsored racing effort. Swede Savage, a talented young driver, drove most of the races for the AAR team in the '70 season.

SCCA rules required at least 2700 production cars be sold to qualify any specialized body parts used on the racecars. That led to the AAR 'Cuda, which reached dealers in late March. They were identified by a flat-black fiberglass hood with a functional scoop. A "strobe" stripe on the side ended with the word "CUDA" and an AAR badge. Limelight was one of seven catchy "High Impact" optional paint colors.

Rear tires were larger than the front rubber and provided an aggressive stance. Dual exhaust pipes exited

in front of the rear wheels. A heavy-duty suspension with a rear antisway bar improved handling.

The new Barracuda now had an engine bay wide enough to hold "big-block" motors up to 440 cid, but for Trans-Am racing, a smaller 340-cid V-8 was used. The series's over-2.0-liter class had a 305-cid limit, but the 340 could be destroked to meet that standard. Racecars had a 440-bhp four-barrel-carbureted V-8. Retail-market cars sprouted three two-barrel Holley carbs on an Edelbrock aluminum manifold that put out a factory-rated 290 bhp—although actual horsepower was said to be around 325.

Buyers could choose a four-speed manual or TorqueFlite automatic transmission, with a Sure-Grip antislip axle. The base price of $3966 was about $800 more than a standard 'Cuda coupe.

In spite of the engineering and expertise behind the Barracuda's racing team, Plymouth finished last in the 1970 Trans-Am standings. Plymouth didn't sponsor a factory team in Trans-Am the next year. The ponycar market was fading and all other makes except AMC pulled their factory sponsorship from Trans-Am racing in 1971. The production AAR 'Cuda died with the racing program.

The AAR 'Cuda might not have made racing history, but the production version was a quick, good-handling ponycar. *Car and Driver* complained of excessive understeer, but other magazines were impressed. *Sports Car Graphic* tested the AAR and covered the quarter-mile in 14.4 seconds at 98.4 mph; 0–60 mph took only six seconds and estimated top speed was 137 mph. Although *Sports Car Graphic* felt the 'Cuda had a firm ride and the engine was rough below 3000 rpm, it went on to say, "But drop down a cog, stomp your foot on a straightaway and get it up in the hills and you'll find little dip, sway or roll, strong, predictable cornering power and, for its size, near-great engine response as those other two Holleys open up for the pull."

Car Life said the AAR 'Cuda was "the Barracuda to buy if you want a road car capable of doing what an enthusiast wants to do on the open road."

1971
Chrysler 300
Hardtop Sedan

The age of full-sized performance cars was effectively over by 1970, eclipsed as they were by the hot intermediate muscle cars. It would fall to Chrysler Corporation to field the last of the sportier leviathans, the 1971 Plymouth Sport Fury GT and Chrysler 300.

The final 300 of the era was a descendant of the so-called Sport Series launched in '62. Having shed the convertible body style after the 1970 model year, it remained available as a two- or four-door hardtop, which started at $4608 and $4687, respectively. The bodies and 124-inch wheelbase were shared with the Chrysler Newport and New Yorker. Clean, uncluttered "fuselage" styling that had been around since 1969 made these Chryslers appear

even more massive than their 224.7-inch length. Ventless front-door glass, formerly found only on two-door hardtops, was now standard throughout the line.

What made the 300 stand out from the rest of the '71 Chrysler lineup? For starters, it was distinguished by hidden headlights and a thin "grille within a grille" composed of bright vertical bars set against a black field. In back, six bright-edged segments sat side by side to create a full-width taillight ensemble. Black-center wheel covers were unique to the series, though finely slotted road wheels were an option. The spacious interior featured standard vinyl bucket seats that reflected the 300's sporting heritage, though a vinyl or cloth-and-vinyl contoured bench seat was available.

In 1969, *Car Life* tested a 300 similar to the car shown here and hit 60 mph in 8.5 seconds, with a top speed of 119 mph. The magazine selected the 300 as the year's "Best Prestige Car," and contended, "The solid ride, the responsive wheel, the logical controls, the combination of minor items, and good basic design made the car into a driver's car, without taking away any creature comfort. The Chrysler 300 boomed down the beach a long time ago, but it still has Daytona sand in its shoes."

Although not a "hemi" of the type that powered the "letter-car" beach blasters of yore, the 440-cid V-8 in late 300s was plenty strong. It put out 335 bhp in 1971 (with 370 optional via dual exhausts and higher compression). Even in a 4321-pound sedan, that was enough to honor 300 tradition.

Chryslers of this era differed from other big American cars in that they had rigid unibodies and torsion-bar front suspension. These factors contributed to the good roadability that impressed the *Car Life* writers. Front disc brakes were optional.

The 300 name would rise again in 1999 as the front-wheel-drive, V-6 midsize 300M. However, the spirit of the originals wasn't fully recaptured until the large, rear-drive 2005–23 model—and its available revived hemi V-8.

1971
Ford Mustang
Convertible Coupe

I
f someone wanted to create the most loaded and potentially collectible 1971 Ford Mustang conceivable, this may be it. If that someone had an inkling that the muscle era was ending and that '71 would be the last year for big-engine Mustangs, they ordered the sort of "ponycar" that would create excitement in the collector-car market decades later.

For starters, the Mustang convertible had the optional "Super Cobra Jet" engine, which was Ford's Cobra Jet 429-cid V-8 with the added Drag Pack that included a high-lift camshaft with longer valve duration; mechanical valve lifters; and adjustable rocker arms, special forged pistons, and high-performance connecting rods secured with cap

screws—all aids in letting the engine rev high. The SCJ's bottom end was supported by four-bolt main bearings in which a modified crankshaft turned. Airflow through the Holley four-barrel carburetor and intake manifold was enhanced by a twin-scoop Ram Air hood with black accents and twist-type latches. So equipped, the Super Cobra Jet was conservatively rated at 375 bhp to placate the insurance industry, but actual output was believed to be considerably more—perhaps well clear of 400 horsepower.

The 429 could be paired with the SelectShift three-speed automatic transmission or a close-ratio four-speed manual gearbox with a Hurst shifter. Only eight 1971 Mustang convertibles (of the 6121 made) were built with the Super

Cobra Jet engine; this is one of only five that had the four-speed.

There was more in store to up the performance potential of this particular car. The nodular rear end has a Detroit Locker differential with a 4.11:1 axle ratio for brisk takeoffs. F60-15 tires are mounted on Ford's Magnum 500 five-spoke chrome wheels. Its other factory options include power front disc brakes, power steering, full instrumentation, power windows (a first-time Mustang extra), console, AM radio/eight-track-tape stereo, Decor Group, and Convenience Group. Grabber Lime paint—one of four vivid Grabber hues—completes the package. With all that, the $3322 base price of this singular car was raised to $5330.

A design team headed by Gale Halderman cooked up the look of the 1971 Mustang. In early 1968, Ford President Semon E. Knudsen approved one of the group's design themes, which was refined into the finished product. Sheetmetal was bulkier than ever, but details like a galloping-horse grille ornament and tri-section taillights linked the new model to its forebears. As before, three body styles were listed: notchback hardtop coupe, fastback hardtop, and a convertible with a power five-ply vinyl top and tempered-glass rear window.

The 1971–73 Mustang was as physically big as Ford's pony ever got. Wheelbase was extended by one inch to 109, but compared to the original mid-Sixties version, it was nearly eight inches longer and almost six inches wider. Big-block engines had been shoehorned into 1967–70 Mustangs, but the '71 had a wider track to better accommodate them. Of course, that was planned during the horsepower-happy late Sixties; times were changing by 1971. The muscle era was ending, and with it went 429-cube Mustangs.

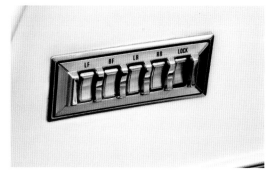

1972
AMC Gremlin X
Two-Door Sedan

merican Motors positioned itself as the nation's small-car leader. AMC knew it couldn't compete head to head in every segment with the Big Three, but money could be made in the compact field, where they typically showed little interest. In the late Sixties, AMC learned that both General Motors and Ford were planning to bring out subcompact import-fighters for 1971. American Motors needed to defend its turf.

However, the company was more strapped for cash than usual, faced as it was with the development costs for the compact Hornet and the impending purchase of Kaiser Jeep. The solution came not from the engineering department, but from styling. Styling chief Dick Teague was used to operating on tight budgets. He learned the trick of creating new looks for old body shells when he worked for Packard in its final years. Now Teague urged building a shortened version of the Hornet that was due out for 1970.

The Hornet then in development had AMC's most up-to-date engineering. By lopping 18 inches off the rear, the compact Hornet became the subcompact Gremlin, and

AMC had a new model for very little investment.

The front half of the car was very much a Hornet. The difference was in the back. The rear looked as if it had been guillotined, and that was its appeal. Love it or hate it, the Gremlin got attention. The chopped rear end was also practical. It provided good cargo room, and the large hatch window was a convenience rarely seen in America at the time.

Inside the car there was also a marked difference between front and rear. The front seat retained its Hornet dimensions, and was wide and roomy for a subcompact.

However, back-seat passengers knew where those 18 inches of length were cut. (*Car and Driver* quipped that "rear legroom is tighter than Nixon's fiscal policy.")

Beneath the sheetmetal, engineering shortened the Hornet's wheelbase from 108 inches to 96. Tried-and-true AMC sixes provided the power (though a V-8 and a four would be added in later years). Fuel economy was in the 20–25-mpg range—not an import-beater, but quite good for a domestic.

The Gremlin made its debut on April Fool's Day, 1970—beating the Chevrolet Vega and Ford Pinto to market by half a year. Prices started at $1879 for a Gremlin without a back seat.

Come 1971, it was possible to get a Gremlin with a sportier look thanks to the "X" option package. Features

were a spear-style bodyside decal, body-color grille surround (with most colors), slotted 14×6 steel wheels, D70×14 Polyglas tires, and a space-saver spare tire. Gremlin X interiors included carpeting, pleated-vinyl bucket seats, and a three-spoke sport steering wheel. The 1972 version of the option group continued virtually unchanged.

Standard power for any '72 Gremlin came from a 232-cid (3.8-liter) six with 100 net bhp—the industry's new, more "realistic" reporting standard. Buyers could select an optional Chrysler-built Torque-Command three-speed automatic transmission and Black was a rare extra-cost paint alternative to the eight standard colors listed for the X.

Gremlin production rose steadily through 1974 (and the first gas crisis), then trailed off until the line's cessation in 1978. There was a Gremlin X all the way to the end.

1972
Oldsmobile
Ninety-Eight
Regency
Hardtop Sedan

Both Oldsmobile and Cadillac celebrated anniversaries in 1972, Cadillac its 70th and Oldsmobile—then the oldest surviving American automaker—its 75th. Both seemingly decided it was the velour anniversary. The fabric had vanished from automobile interiors after World War II, but thanks to the leads of Olds and Cadillac, velour became the number-one upholstery choice for American cars in the Seventies.

Oldsmobile's velour seat had a pillowed effect that made it look like an extremely inviting couch. This plush-sofa look was also widely copied during the Seventies. Olds had just created one of the hallmarks of the exuberant luxury that Americans of that era craved.

This trendsetting interior made its debut in the Ninety-Eight Regency four-door hardtop, a midyear '72 model with a production run capped at 5000 units (though it appears 2650 were made). The front seat was a 60/40 design with separate power adjustments for driver and passenger. Oldsmobile didn't stop there with the special touches. Tiffany & Co., the New York jeweler, styled the face of the Regency's dashboard clock and provided a sterling-silver key ring. Every Regency was sprayed in Tiffany Gold metallic paint, but the interior came in a choice of black or gold.

On the surface, there was little more a Ninety-Eight buyer could want. Still, it was possible to add things like an eight-track tape player and an external thermometer mounted on the driver's door.

John Beltz, Oldsmobile's general manager from 1969 to 1972, said Olds buyers didn't want small cars, which the Ninety-Eight certainly wasn't—not with a 127-inch wheelbase and an overall length of 228 inches. Of course, he said this before the 1973–74 OPEC oil embargo, at a time when most Americans weren't yet overly concerned with fuel economy. During that crisis, many of those Olds buyers had the opportunity to reexamine their feelings about small cars while waiting in line for rationed gasoline.

The 1972 Regency had a 455-cid V-8 of 225 or 250 net bhp (the latter with dual exhausts) to move its roughly 5100 pounds, and it moved them well. A similar '71 Ninety-Eight did 0–60 mph in 8.7 seconds (but averaged only 11 mpg) in *Motor Trend* testing. In a comparison test with a Buick Electra and a Mercury Marquis, *MT* was impressed by the Ninety-Eight's ride and handling. "The big surprise was Olds," it said. "The ride was soft and comfortable as the Electra's but the cornering exceeded that of the Marquis." *Motor Trend* went on to state, "Of the three cars tested, the nod has to go to the Olds 98, for superiority of ride and handling."

Olds realized it was on to a good thing and brought back the Regency as a regular model for '73, selling 34,009 of them. The following year saw the addition of a two-door Regency. The name was destined to remain a part of the Ninety-Eight family until that line was discontinued in 1996, and then it transferred to the Eighty-Eight range through '98.

1973
Cadillac Coupe de Ville Hardtop Coupe

When General Motors put the first publicly available "hardtop convertibles" on sale in summer 1949, it named the three pioneers of the body style in romantic overtones. There was the Oldsmobile 98 Holiday, Buick Roadmaster Riviera, and the Cadillac Series 62 Coupe de Ville. Like the original, the hardtop Coupe de Villes that followed over the next 24 years forged a mix of formal elegance and sporty vivacity.

Coupe de Villes were consistently trimmed in high-fashion fabrics. The model's premium price also covered more standard features than Cadillac's lower-priced hardtop variants. Each new rendition would be a siren song calling to thousands of well-heeled Americans.

Judging by raw numbers alone, that allure was never greater than in 1973. No fewer than 112,849 luxury-car shoppers plunked down at least $6268 to get one—the most to that point in the nameplate's history. It was the single-most popular Caddy of that model year (something that had happened for the Coupe de Ville only once before, in 1963), and it alone accounted for 37 percent of the record 304,839 Cadillacs produced as '73s.

It also happened to be the last time that the Coupe de Ville was rendered as a true pillarless hardtop. Though the 1974 job was built from the same basic architecture, it adopted a "B" pillar and fixed quarter windows, and that's how Coupe de Villes would be constructed through 1993. Close to 1 million hardtops were made from '49 to '73.

The 1973 Cadillac "standards" in the Calais, De Ville, and Fleetwood series had their start with the complete redo ordained for 1971. Wheelbase stretched out 0.5 inch

to 130 inches for the C-body Calais and De Ville. By '73, when a new federal bumper-impact standard prompted a stouter front bumper that was designed with some fore-and-aft "give," overall length reached 228.5 inches. The annual facelift incorporated a blunter hood and a flatter grille.

Motive power was still produced by a 472-cid V-8 of 220 net bhp, channeled through a Turbo Hydra-Matic automatic transmission. These powerteam elements rested in a perimeter frame that had been redesigned for the '71-generation Caddy.

Nineteen seventy-three Coupe de Ville seats saw a switch to a pattern of narrowed pleats and more-distinctly pillowed upper sections. Two kinds of interior fabrics were available, and leather upholstery was available in 12 color combinations. Door and quarter-panel coverings featured a new "soft pillow" appearance.

1973
Plymouth
Duster 340 Coupe

The type of Plymouth Duster shown on these pages is precisely the kind for which the Duster was created in the first place. The vast majority of the more than 1.3 million people who bought a Duster between 1970 and '76 procured a stylish but essentially economical compact car. However, the small circle of people who brought it into being were primarily motivated to come up with a budget "bomb" to outrun Chevrolet Novas with "small-block" V-8 engines. The tool for that job was the Duster 340.

Product planners had $15 million at their disposal to freshen up the sensible but dowdy Valiant compact for 1970. Nobody told them they could spend that money to create a slick, new vehicle—but then, nobody said they *couldn't*. Opting to design first and tell the bosses about it later, they conjured a coupe with fastback overtones that took advantage of Valiant's existing 108-inch-wheelbase

platform, yet could serve as an attractive wrapper for the affordable performance car they had in mind. (The '70 Valiant still got its needed update via various appearance and engineering features carried over from the Duster.)

Like other Mopars, it had Unibody construction and torsion-bar front suspension. Base models were available with the "bulletproof" inline Slant Six or a 318-cid V-8. The Duster 340 was an economy muscle car with a standard 340-cube V-8 with four-barrel carburetor and 10.5:1 compression ratio that made 275 gross bhp at introduction. It was lighter and less expensive than a Barracuda with the same engine, so the Duster 340 was faster and more popular than its glamorous "ponycar" compatriot.

The Duster was due for a freshening of its own by 1973. The hood gained a raised center section. Stylist Jeffrey Godshall penned a new grille consisting of stacks of argent

rectangular boxes that were filled with an eggcrate pattern and flanked by rectangular headlamp doors. A deeper front bumper addressed the new federal standards. Redone taillights framed in bright bezels replaced the frameless "slit" lamps found on earlier cars. The 340 sported new standard stripe designs on the bodysides and tail panel.

Beginning in '72, the compression in the 340-cube V-8 was pushed back to 8.5:1, all the better to accept no- and low-lead fuel. Under the new net-horsepower reporting, it put out 240 bhp. However, Duster 340 retained its midget-muscle credentials with features like dual exhausts, a heavy-duty suspension, and 5.5×14 wheels shod with 70-series tires, all for $2822. TorqueFlite automatic transmission and a four-speed stickshift were extra-cost alterna-

tives to the standard floor-shift three-speed manual. This car's rare, oversized 26-inch-radiator option no doubt came in handy for handling the extra-cost air conditioning.

The Duster struck a chord with the public and Plymouth ran off 217,192 of them in the first year—more than four times the number of Valiant sedans. By '73, Duster demand was just shy of 265,000. Of those, 15,731 were Duster 340s.

Six-cylinder Dusters and Valiants were popular amid the OPEC oil embargo. In '74, a 360-cube engine rated at 245 bhp replaced the 340, but high-priced fuel and stiff insurance rates tamped down the lure of performance cars. The Duster and Valiant lasted until 1976, when they were replaced by the ill-fated Plymouth Volaré.

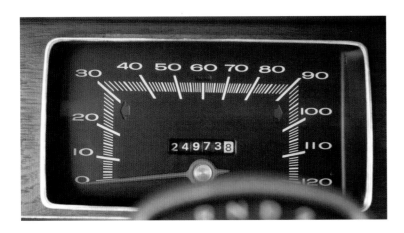

1974
Ford LTD Country Squire Station Wagon

It may surprise the modern reader, but into the early Seventies, traditional full-sized cars held sway as the sales leaders in most American manufacturers' product mixes. Then came the OPEC oil embargo of October 1973 to March 1974, and the big "standards" were shunned in favor of smaller cars with better fuel mileage, a good many of them imports.

The '74 model-year production totals for the "land yachts" were brutal. A quick sample: Chrysler and Oldsmobile receded by almost exactly half from the year before. Ford was down by 46 percent. It was that kind of year for practically all the domestic brands.

Barring the geopolitical fallout from war in the Middle East, things might not have been any-where as bleak in Dearborn. The 1974 Fords were modestly changed follow-ups to the all-new '73 models that enticed more than 850,000 orders. Evolved, but fresh, sheetmetal appeared below the beltline, grilles and taillights were

redone in familiar themes, and an updated instrument panel featured controls that were more logically placed. Underneath was a new frame with five cross members and a rear suspension modified for better ride and handling. For '74, grille detailing was tweaked and rear bumpers were brought up to the same body-damage-resistance standard already in place for front bumpers.

In more years than not, Ford led in station wagon sales. By 1974 the clear favorite in its showrooms was the Country Squire, which stood out with its simulated-wood trim that recalled the long-gone "woody" era.

In terms of equipment, the Squire was the wagon equivalent of the high-volume LTD series, and the '74 model gained the stand-up hood ornament and standard steel-belted-radial tires added to that line.

However, while a 351-cid V-8 was the base engine in other big Fords, the Country Squire (and the LTD Special without faux-wood décor) were newly bestowed with a 176-bhp 400-cube engine as standard. The top power option of the year was a 460 V-8 with 200 horsepower.

Ford station wagons came in a choice of six-passenger or eight-passenger seating, the latter with inward-facing dual rear seats for $120 more. Six-seaters had additional load space under the main cargo floor. The wagons also featured the Ford-pioneered "Magic Doorgate" that worked as a drop-down tailgate or side-hinged door.

Country Squires were the priciest big Fords, starting at $4898 for the six-passenger model. Demand came to 64,067, a 44.8-percent loss from 1973. Yes, it was that kind of year.

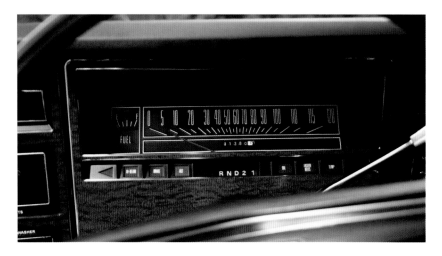

1976
Buick
Riviera Coupe

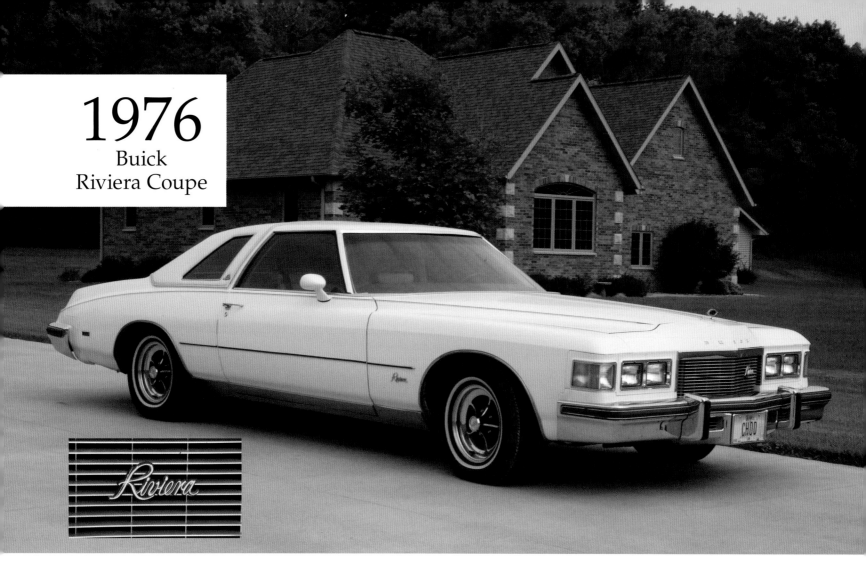

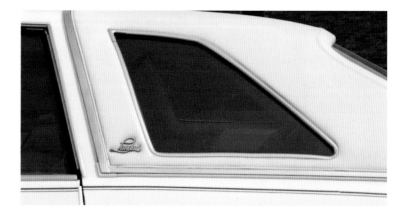

While it might be harsh, and possibly even incorrect, to call the appearance of the 1974–76 Buick Riviera "bland," there is no denying that the look was much more conventional than the one it replaced: the 1971–73 version that left potential customers to question whether they loved or hated its daring "boattail" design.

General Motors Design Vice President Bill Mitchell wanted to make a dramatic statement with the third-generation Riviera scheduled for the '71 model year. He got the Buick studio responsible for large-car designs to give him one with a tapering "greenhouse" that came to a pronounced point in the trunklid and rear bumper. But what's delightfully daring to one set of eyes can be outlandish to another. Demand through '73 hovered around 34,000 units per year, the worst in the Riviera's history, while the Cadillac Eldorado and Oldsmobile Toronado that used the same GM "E" body were seeing much better sales. The boattail styling was identified as a problem.

The big Riviera (its 122-inch wheelbase was the longest that would ever be used by the personal-luxury Buick) was planned to run through 1976. From '74 on it would do so with a notchback roofline that was in line with the big-bucks personal coupes then on the market. A squared-up, slab-sided lower body did away with the swoopy, dipped "hips" of the previous Riviera. The trunk pushed up above a sloping sculpture line in the rear quarters—almost a preview of the what was to come on the "trunkback" 1980 Cadillac Seville. (If nothing else, the rear end made it easier to incorporate a rear bumper engineered to meet the new federal five-mph impact standard.)

The roof had wide B-pillars and fixed opera windows. It could be dressed with an optional full vinyl top or a Landau treatment with bright-edged padded vinyl applied over the B-pillars and rear half of the roof.

Fully open wheel arches and a long hood were retained, but the front fascia became fully upright, abandoning the aggressive forward lean of the 1971–73 cars. In 1975, rectangular headlights came into use. That same year saw a shift to a flat-faced dashboard with full-width woodgrain trim in the lower half.

The 1976 Riv was freshened with a grille mesh of closely aligned horizontal bars complemented by nine thin uprights. The only engine available was Buick's 455-cid V-8. Rated at 205 net bhp, it was appearing for the last time.

Caught up in the oil-embargo chaos that shriveled sales of large cars in 1974, just 20,129 Rivieras were built, and demand slid to 17,306 the next year as the industry's pain persisted. Just 20,082 of the '76s rolled out.

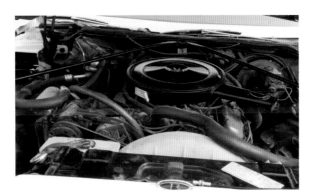

1976
Ford Gran Torino Coupe

The time is the mid Seventies. The place, if that word can be applied to a fictional locale, is the mean streets of Bay City, California. The men of the hour are young police detectives David Starsky and Kenneth Hutchinson—Starsky and Hutch to their associates. Their able crime-fighting partner is the "striped tomato," a vibrantly red 1974 Ford Gran Torino coupe boldly emblazoned with a white "horseshoe" over the roof and sides.

Never underestimate the power of image. The 1972–76 Torino might have gone down as just another mass-market intermediate if not for what started on April 30, 1975. The American Broadcasting Company aired the 90-minute premiere of *Starsky and Hutch*, prelude to its becoming an hour-long weekly television series for more than four years. In no time, the striped tomato was part of popular culture and the Torino became a car for young boys to lust after.

This could have been the spark of a great marketing opportunity for Ford. Unfortunately, the timing wasn't ideal since it was already planning to move on from the Torino. Still, the buzz could not be ignored. What to do?

In March 1976, Ford's assembly plant in Chicago began rolling out replicas of the TV car. The 1000 copies made captured the iconic red hue and white stripe fairly accurately. However, the retail examples lacked the Hollywood car's slotted alloy wheels, the like of which Ford did not offer or even try to duplicate. (That did not stop the owners of the car shown from outfitting theirs with aftermarket wheels and a police radio to better channel the aura of the "television star.")

Torinos of this generation were quite different from the Fairlanes and Torinos that preceded them. After a decade of unitized construction, midsized Fords switched to a body-on-frame architecture. The perimeter frame with five cross members was said to be a boon to on-road quiet, but looming vehicle-safety regulations were a more direct reason for the change. A shift to coil springs and four-link geometry for the rear suspension sacrificed handling for a softer, quieter ride as the Torino attempted to appeal to big-car owners.

They were bigger cars, too. While two-door models retreated to a 114-inch wheelbase, four-door sedans and station wagons were on a 118-inch span that was one inch longer than before for sedans and four inches greater for wagons. Ford advertised that the new Torinos were "a little heavier and a little wider." Interior dimensions were increased.

What Torinos weren't, as time went on, was sportier. There was a fastback hardtop for the first couple of years and a version badged Sport through 1975, though it gradually devolved into a package of appearance items and full instrumentation. In the era of oil embargoes and stricter tailpipe-emissions regulations, by 1976 output of the V-8s was down to 154 bhp in the standard 351-cid job, 180 in the 400-incher, and 202 for the 460.

Torino wrested intermediate-sales bragging rights from the Chevrolet Chevelle in the generation's early years. Then the Oldsmobile Cutlass surged ahead of them both. In '77, an LTD II replaced the Torino.

1977
Oldsmobile
Toronado XSR Coupe

On the pages devoted to the Toronado XSR in a 1977 catalog, Oldsmobile asked, "Can we build one for you?" It turns out the automaker meant exactly that—one.

The XSR was a '77 Toronado sent to American Sunroof Corporation (ASC) for a T-top conversion. This was no typical conversion, but a power T-top with glass panels that slid under a wide center bar.

Oldsmobile scheduled the car for serial production and had high hopes for it. Not only did an airbrushed XSR share the cover of the '77 Olds "big-car" brochure, but it was touted on a two-page spread within. Ultimately, however, the top mechanism was judged to be too troublesome, so the only XSR ever built was the Firethorn Red prototype.

Instead, Olds produced the Toronado XS, an XSR with a conventional tinted-glass sunroof in place of the T-top. Both shared an unusual wraparound rear window often compared to Studebaker Starlight coupes. Using hot-bent-wire technology to form sharp corners, the glass

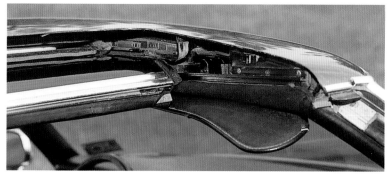

wrapped from B-pillar to B-pillar. Otherwise, the XS and, for that matter, the XSR, were standard Toronados.

When the division downsized its Eighty-Eights and Ninety-Eights in 1977, Toronado became the biggest Oldsmobile, weighing at least 4747 pounds and with an overall length of 227.5 inches. The 455-cid V-8 of yore was replaced by a 200-bhp, 403-cid V-8. The XS sold for $10,684, or $2550 more than a base Toronado Brougham. Production in the first year came to 2713; another 2453 were made for '78.

Had the XSR worked out as intended, it would have been another interesting chapter in the history of the Tornado. Introduced in 1966, it was the first front-wheel-drive American car since the 1937 Cord. The second generation of the E-body personal-luxury coupe bowed for 1971 (and

ran to '78) with styling that was more formal. Eye-level brake and signal lamps below the rear window predicted the required high-level stop lamps first seen in the Eighties.

ASC bought back the lone XSR in 1978. It hoped to sell other manufacturers on the "electric, self-storing T-top" idea, but gave that up by 1981. The XSR was then sold and disappeared into the used-car market.

After some time, the unique Toronado was exiled to a Virginia pasture, where it sat rusting until 1994. Word of its existence passed through the Oldsmobile enthusiast community, a member of which purchased the car and had it restored. According to a subsequent owner, the T-top Toro is something of a fair-weather friend because the prototype mechanism lacks a drain and leaks in the rain.

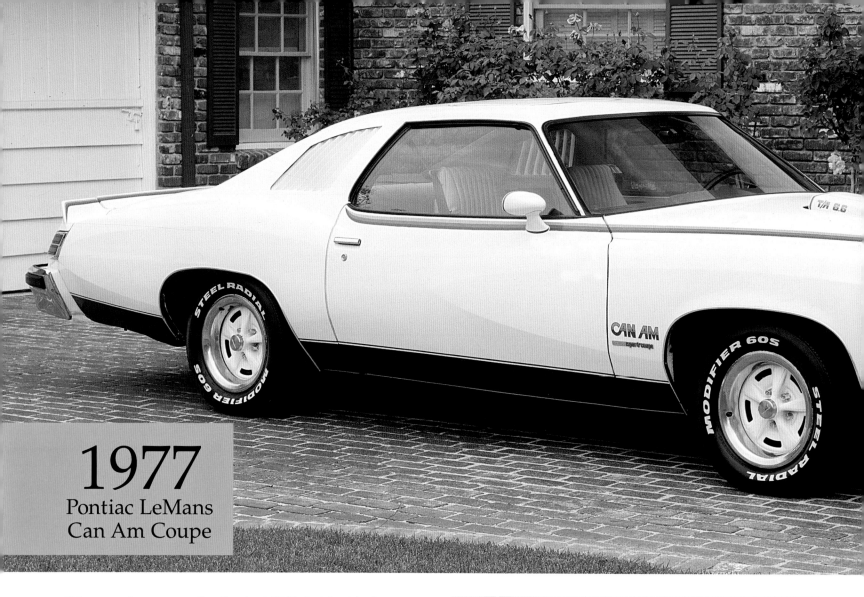

1977
Pontiac LeMans
Can Am Coupe

t was a few years after the last GTO, but just before "downsizing." It was in between fuel crises. It was 1977, the year when Pontiac saw a brief window of opportunity—more like a peephole in retrospect—to reinject some performance vitality in its midsize LeMans.

The finished product was a tall-tailed coupe with Firebird Trans Am punch under its hood and appearance and handling enhancements sprinkled liberally throughout. Pontiac christened it the Can Am.

Three things made the Can Am possible. The first was the arrival of a 200-bhp 400-cid V-8 for the 1977 Trans Am, where it quickly became a hit. The second was the memory of a Pontiac show car from '74, the All-American, which featured striking white paint (with matching wheels) and a tall rear spoiler. The third was a little push from an old friend of Pontiac management, Jim Wangers.

Wangers, a creator of the GTO, was now with a Detroit-based conversion company that had worked up mid-Seventies sporty cars for other manufacturers. He suggested a sort of updated GTO Judge to Pontiac General Manager

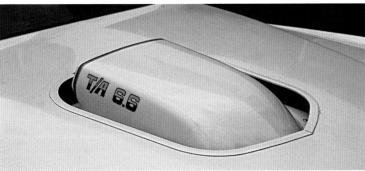

Alex Mair. Intrigued, Mair had John Schinella's design team have a go at it. The designers adapted ideas from the All-American to the '77 LeMans Sport Coupe, engineers mixed in beefier running gear and the T/A engine, and Wangers' firm fabricated the hood "shaker," spoiler, and decals.

The high-performance 400 (a 185-horse 403 was installed for California-bound and high-altitude cars) was mated to a three-speed automatic transmission. Also included in the $5419 base price were power front disc brakes, variable-ratio power steering, front and rear stabilizers, and Pontiac's Rally RTS handling package teamed with GR780-15 steel-belted-radial tires. *Car and Driver* found the Can Am's 17.2-second quarter-mile time "decent" and its cornering "excellent . . . by any sedan standard."

The Cameo White paint and red/orange/yellow graphics were augmented by blackout trim, twin sport mirrors, and Rally II wheels. A Grand Prix-style dash with a full gauge cluster kept drivers informed. Any of the 1337 owners who wanted more for their car could select extras like a sunroof, bucket seats, power windows, and air conditioning.

Among the curious "one and done" cars of the Seventies is the 1978 Plymouth Volaré Super Coupe. It flared briefly to bestow a muscular mood on the car that had the weighty task of replacing the time-worn Valiant.

Volaré bowed for 1976, was sold with the Valiant and Duster for a season, then took over as the sole Plymouth compact through 1980. It and the similar Dodge Aspen won the *Motor Trend* Car of the Year Award in '76 but fell prey to numerous recalls.

These F-body cars came as a coupe, a four-door sedan, and a station wagon that was a rarity among domestic compacts. Wheelbases were split—108.7 inches for the two-door; 112.7 for the others—and the chassis included a new take on Chrysler's front torsion bars. Two L-shaped bars were mounted laterally ahead of the engine, the shorter legs pointed back toward a lower suspension arm and acting like a lever that longitudinally located the arm and provided springing action for better ride and quiet.

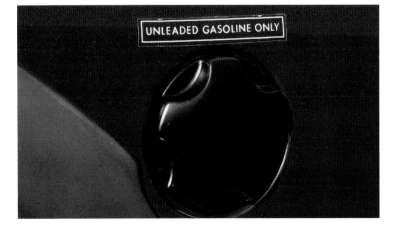

Ostensibly an economy car, the Volaré could still be purchased somewhat plush or, as it turned out, sporty. Right off the bat in '76 it became the new address for the Road Runner nameplate, and there were additional packages to make the Runner look a little hairier. Then in '78 along came the Super Coupe.

An extra-cost option group for the $3905 Volaré V-8 coupe, the Super Coupe coated the car in Crimson Sunfire Metallic and Flat Black paints. Yellow Orange, Brite Orange, and Dark Red stripes were teamed to provide a pop of color on the sides, up the B-pillars, and over the roof. As with the Road Runner Sport Pak group, the Super Coupe came with a set of horizontal louvers applied over each rear-quarter window, deep front air dam and decklid spoiler, and fender flares—though the Super's flares were a little meatier. Dual racing mirrors and a package-specific five-arm gas cap completed the look.

Mechanically, the Super Coupe featured a heavy-duty suspension with rear sway bar. Rolling stock—deep, slotted 15×8-inch road wheels wrapped in GR60×15 white-letter tires—was shared with the rare Street Kit Car package, yet *another* type of performance-oriented Volaré. Under the hood was the biggest V-8 available in the compact, a 360-cid "small block" with a four-barrel carburetor. In 49-state tune, it made 175 bhp and incorporated Chrysler's Lean Burn combustion system that strove to raise fuel economy. (A 160-horse non-Lean Burn 360 served in California and high-altitude areas.) The TorqueFlite automatic was the only available transmission.

Buyers needn't have stopped with the package as it was. They could order things like a three-spoke "Tuff" steering wheel; floor console; and Premier interior with vinyl bucket seats, shag carpeting, woodgrain dash trim, and more.

A dwindling number of Road Runners were made through 1980. The Super Coupe, though, was one and done.

1979
Buick LeSabre Sport Coupe

Buick may have made its traditional big family cars considerably smaller for the late Seventies, but they were still Buicks. One persistent bow to brand history in that period was the inclusion of a "banker's hot rod," the LeSabre Sport Coupe.

This was the latest incarnation of the idea behind the Century, Invicta, and Wildcat of years past. It made use of two of the division's other enthusiasms: a V-6 engine and turbocharging.

The first thing to notice about this LeSabre is its packaging. Foreseeing a future for smaller, more efficient cars, General Motors undertook an across-the-board downsizing of its 1977 full-sized models. In the case of the B-body LeSabre coupe and four-door sedan, this resulted in weight reductions of up to 665 pounds. Wheelbase was condensed by 8.1 inches (to 115.9 inches) and the cars were considerably shorter and narrower overall, even as interior headroom and legroom improved from the truly large cars they replaced.

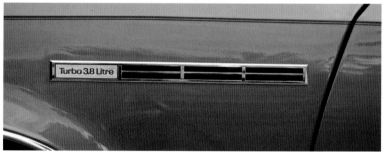

Standard engine for the new-age LeSabres was a 3.8-liter (231-cid) V-6 descended from the very 90-degree-angle unit Buick first cooked up for its senior-compact Special in 1962. Buick sold rights and tooling to the engine to Kaiser-Jeep in 1967, then bought them back in 1974 in time to place the V-6 in certain '75 models.

Right away Buick engineers began tinkering with turbocharging in pursuit of V-8-like power with better fuel economy. Come '78, the division was ready to put cars with turbo V-6s on sale. One of them was the LeSabre Sport Coupe.

The Sport Coupe actually launched in 1977 with a selection of three V-8s. Its basic package included a firmed-up suspension, quicker steering, upsized front disc brakes, chrome-plated road wheels with GR70-15 whitewall tires, and blackout trim. *Car and Driver* was amazed at how well Buick got the Sport Coupe's "cornering ability close to that of a [Mercedes-Benz] 450SE on the skidpad."

In '78 the car was endowed with a choice of turbo V-6s: 150 bhp with two-barrel carburetor or 165 horsepower with four-throat carb. *Road & Track* said of the latter, "Overall, the turbocharged Buick V-6 engine works quite well, providing acceptable performance with improved fuel economy."

Only the four-barrel engine was used in 1979, and it was boosted to 170 bhp. Bucket seats and a console were new options for the 3582 Sport Coupes made. The hotted-up LeSabre lasted until '80, but the turbo V-6 was hardly done.

1979
Chevrolet Camaro
Berlinetta Coupe

The Chevrolet Camaro Berlinetta was a true product of the Seventies. The second-generation Camaro was introduced in early 1970, when the muscle car era was at its apex and Chevrolet's sporty "ponycar" offered high-performance big-block-V-8 and Z28 models. However, rising insurance rates, tightening emissions standards, and then the OPEC oil embargo soon brought an end to the performance era within a few years. Car buyers, in turn, began placing more importance on luxury than speed. Personal-luxury cars charged in to fill the void.

For 1973, Camaro responded to the trend toward luxury with a new LT (Luxury Touring) model. In place of go-fast gear it packed in more sound insulation and nicer interior trim. The LT proved popular and for 1979 it was rebadged Berlinetta with an added chrome grille, pinstriping, deeply contoured front bucket seats, plush headliner, dual horns, and a more isolating suspension. (The name traced its

roots back to a '73 Camaro clay styling study which morphed into a 1977 auto-show car that predicted the '78 Camaro's freshened frontal styling.)

Standard in base and Berlinetta engine bays was a 250-cid inline six rated at 115 bhp. The top engine was a 350-cid V-8 that made 170 bhp in base and Berlinetta models or 175 bhp in the Z28. Seen here is the middle choice, a 305-cid V-8 with a two-barrel carburetor. It produced 130 bhp at 3200 rpm and 245 pound-feet of torque at 2000 rpm. This 5.0-liter engine was available with a three-speed automatic transmission or a four-speed manual.

Berlinetta was a good choice for those who sought luxury in a car that was still sporty with good handling. Advertising reminded buyers that it was still a "hugger"—as early Camaros had been promoted. However, though luxury was king in the late Seventies, the 67,236 plush Berlinettas were outsold by the fast (for the era) Z28.

The 1979 Camaro was still a second-generation car. When introduced in '70, Camaro (and its Pontiac Firebird sibling) drew rave reviews. *Car and Driver* called it "a car of exceptional handling—probably the best that Detroit has ever produced." *Road & Track* enthused, "[W]e'll have to say it's the best American car we've ever driven, and more importantly it's one of the most satisfying for all-around use we've ever driven."

The reason for this praise was the care that Chevrolet engineers put into suspension design. The front suspension was new and the variable-ratio steering gear was moved in front of the ball joints. In the rear, the unusual Nova-sourced single-leaf springs used by the 1967–69 first-generation Camaros were replaced by conventional multileaf springs. Braking was via front discs and rear drums. This fine engineering was wrapped in a low, sleek body that was commonly compared to Ferraris.

1979
Mercury Cougar XR-7 Coupe

W hen one door closes another door opens," Alexander Graham Bell once said—and the inventor of the telephone never even saw a personal-luxury coupe from the Seventies.

With the peak days of high-performance muscle cars and "ponycars" reached by 1970, the next focus of aspirational car buyers became personal coupes. Initially the province of costly specials like the Ford Thunderbird, Buick Riviera, and a few others, other brands were tempted to enter the field with more-affordable "luxury" models wrung from existing midsize cars. When Mercury cashiered its Cougar ponycar after 1973, it retained the name of its plushest version—XR-7—for a new personal coupe derived from the intermediate two-door Montego. A few effective styling distinctions and a deep dive into the Montego parts bin for an ample standard-equipment complement resulted in solid success for the 1974–76 Cougar XR-7.

A follow-up was due for 1977—a year in which the Montego was renamed Cougar. The XR-7 and lesser Cougars used the same body-on-frame construction and all-coil-spring suspension found on intermediate Mercs since 1972, but would wear styling that was more linear and flatter on the sides. There would be an attempt to make the Cougar XR-7 stand apart from the others.

The bulk of that change happened on top and in back. The XR-7 had its own opera-window style with a louver detail and a standard padded-vinyl landau top. Horizontal taillights and a decklid with a Lincoln Continental-like hump were further visual cues. In 1979, the grille finally got its own treatment with four groups of vertical bars (instead of six in other Cougars) framed by body-color dividers.

XR-7s came with an enhanced list of standard equipment. Interiors featured walnut woodgrain appliqués, Flight Bench seats, a deluxe steering wheel, electric clock, and additional sound insulation. The 15-inch wheels had distinct wheel covers (though other choices were available). A dual-note horn and rear stabilizer bar were thrown in, too. A Chamois Decor Group option in 1978–79 delivered a vinyl top, side moldings, striping, polycast wheels, padded-vinyl trunklid face, and interior trim in Chamois tan.

Throughout the 1977–79 run a 5.0-liter (302-cid) V-8 with automatic transmission was standard, but by '79 the only step-up option was a 5.8-liter (351-cid) engine. In fact, the bigger powerplant was required for cars sold in California.

The late Seventies proved to be a boom time for American personal-luxury cars. Most nameplates in the class posted all-time-best sales years. As for the Cougar XR-7, the 124,799 made for 1977 marked a 49-percent jump from the year before, and the 166,508 in '78 and 163,716 in '79 were the two highest model-year totals ever recorded by any Mercury named Cougar.

1979
Pontiac Firebird Trans Am Coupe

During its first 10 years on the market, the Firebird Trans Am took performance-minded drivers for quite a ride. All the while, Pontiac's thoroughbred "pony-car" had been on a breathtaking sales gallop of its own.

From humble beginnings in 1969 of just 705 units (including a scant eight convertibles), the Trans Am only slowly took hold in its early years. It wasn't until 1974 that it cracked 10,000 sales for a model year, but then the gains came fast and furiously, flying in the face of a general withering of the performance-car market. By 1979 the T/A was good for 117,108 examples, or 55.4 percent of all that year's Firebirds. The car's acceptance was an achievement worth celebrating, and Pontiac certainly did—with a distinctive 10th Anniversary Edition.

The commemorative was hard to miss with its two-tone-silver paint, red accent stripes, and a larger than normal rendering of the T/A's signature "screaming chicken" graphic spread-eagle across the hood. Raised white-letter 225/70R15 tires clung to specific 15-inch-diameter slotted, deep-dish alloy wheels. Driver and passengers settled themselves into a cabin finished in silver leather beneath a T-top roof with removable tinted-glass panels.

Anniversary models sold anywhere but in California and high-altitude locales called upon the 400-cid "T/A 6.6" (for its metric displacement) V-8. With a four-barrel carburetor under the "shaker" intake scoop and 8.1:1 compression, it made 220 bhp at 4000 rpm and 320 pound-feet of torque at 2800 revs. A four-speed manual was the mandatory transmission; final drive was through a 3.23:1 gearset.

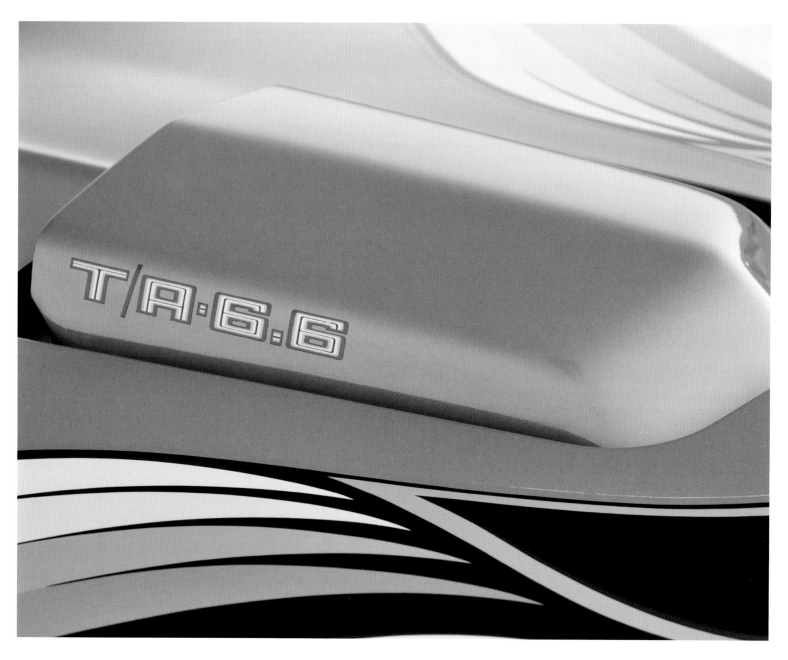

California and altitude cars had to stick with the Oldsmobile-built 403-cube V-8 standard in all other Trans Ams. Possessed of a 7.9:1 compression ratio, its output figures were 185 horsepower at 3600 rpm and 320 pound-feet at 2200. This powerplant came with the three-speed Turbo Hydra-matic automatic.

Naturally, 10th Anniversary cars had all the core Trans Am features. Chin and deck spoilers were accompanied by air deflectors around the wheel openings; air extractors popped out of the front fenders. The dual exhausts terminated in bright twin-pipe splitters. The chassis employed Pontiac's Rally RTS suspension and power assisted brakes—front discs and rear drums. Inside was a padded three-spoke steering wheel with drilled arms, a full array of

gauges in an instrument panel trimmed with a face plate of engine-turned metal, and a console nestled between the bucket seats.

The 1979 Firebird was still a second-generation F-body car, a design introduced in 1970 (and due to run until 1981). Since then it countenanced a number of appearance changes. For '79, the twin grilles—a Pontiac styling cue for 20 years—sank low in a new sloped nose panel that housed deep-set quad headlights. Trans Am and Formula models adopted taillights covered in opaque black plastic for a custom look.

In late January, Pontiac announced that the 10th Anniversary Edition would make its public debut at the 1979 Chicago Auto Show scheduled to open on February 24. However, anyone who attended the Daytona 500 on February 8 got a sneak peak because one of the specials served as the official pace car for the race.

Priced at $10,620—making it the first five-figures Firebird—the 10th Anniversary Edition cost $3737 more than a "regular" Trans Am. By design, Pontiac ran off 7500 of them, counted within the overall run of T/As.

The Firebird was at its peak. It continued through two more generations until 2002. There would be Trans Ams to the end, but never again a sales force like in 1979.

1980
Chrysler New
Yorker Fifth
Avenue Edition
Four-Door Sedan

With U.S. automakers facing a regulatory future that included increasing fuel-mileage targets—a government reaction to the panic of the 1973–74 oil embargo—the wisdom of General Motors's program of shrinking the size of its cars starting in 1977 couldn't be denied. Any manufacturer that wished to remain in the full-size segment came up with scaled-down models at the first opportunity.

For Ford, Mercury, Dodge, and Chrysler, that opportunity came with the 1979 model year. (Lincoln and Plymouth completed the swing to smaller in 1980.) But number-three Chrysler Corporation was struggling financially. To downsize its big cars, it turned to repurposing the unitized B-body platform used by 1971–78 Plymouth and Dodge intermediates. One inch was added to the erstwhile midsizers' sedan/wagon wheelbase for a 118.5-inch span and designers sketched out sharply creased sheetmetal. For the Chrysler-brand cars, they hoped to convey a traditional prestige look even though the vehicles were up to 9.5 inches shorter and 900 pounds lighter than the '78s.

Available only as four-door sedans, these were considered R-body cars. Chryslers came in two series, entry-level Newport and tonier New Yorker. They had different front

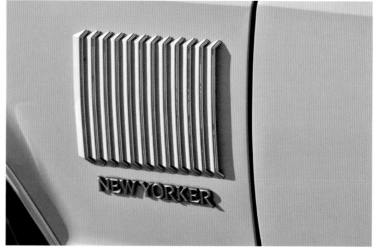

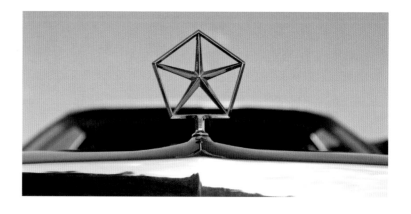

and rear styling, particularly the New Yorker's hidden head-lights, and the Newport came with a standard six-cylinder engine while the New Yorker had a V-8. However, the New Yorker was the basis for a somewhat plusher "option model" known as the Fifth Avenue Edition.

The Fifth Avenue's inside story was this: Light Champagne leather upholstery, leather-wrapped steering wheel on a tilt column, imitation driftwood appliqués, 20-ounce cut-pile carpeting, and additional warning and courtesy lights. External marks were a unique cream-and-beige paint scheme, simulated front-fender louvers, padded landau vinyl roof, edge-lighted rear-quarter windows, pen-tastar hood ornament and trunk-lock cover, color-keyed bumper guards/rub strips, wire wheel covers, and gold-striped whitewall tires.

Though changes to the 1980 R-body Chryslers were virtu-ally undetectable, the New Yorker added air conditioning to its list of standard equipment, and the 360-cid V-8 moved to the options list, replaced by a two-barrel-carbureted 318 that made 120 bhp. (California cars got a four-barrel 318.) Meanwhile, the Fifth Avenue Edition added a second color choice, Black Walnut Metallic with a matching reptile-grain vinyl top. The gold stripe came off the tires but intermittent windshield wipers were a new package feature—and the price of the option was cut by $200 to $1300.

Unfortunately for the Chrysler-Plymouth Division, the bot-tom fell out of demand for R-body Chryslers, which were dogged by quality issues, swooning by 78.5 percent from '79. Orders for the Fifth Avenue Edition were off by about as much. A final run of facelifted '81s fared even worse.

1981
DeLorean
DMC-12 Coupe

C ould the DeLorean have been the Tucker of the
Eighties? Both were the brainchildren of men with
experience in the auto industry who wanted to create
groundbreaking automobiles. Both founders ran up against
the law, tried on federal charges of which they were acquit-
ted—but only after the fast failure of their enterprises.

That's about as far as the similarities go. Unlike Preston
Tucker, John Z. DeLorean could have been a Detroit pooh-
bah had he wanted. After serving as general manager for
Pontiac and Chevrolet, DeLorean rose to a vice presidency
at General Motors. But he was uncomfortable there, view-
ing himself as a hip, round peg not well fitted to GM's
"square" holes, and so he left in 1973.

Two years later he founded the DeLorean Motor Company
with the intention to manufacture an "ethical" car that
would be fun to drive, safe, and durable. It took a while—
much longer than expected—but production finally began in
January 1981 at a plant in Northern Ireland, thanks to a
hand from the UK government.

The car that DeLorean was able to produce there, the
DMC-12, was an attention-getting two-seat coupe with a

stainless-steel-skinned body and gullwing doors, penned by Giorgetto Giugiaro of ItalDesign. At 168 inches long (on a 94.8-inch wheelbase), it stood just 44.9 inches high. Engineering input from Lotus resulted in a central "backbone" frame and fully independent suspension.

A Wankel rotary engine was on DeLorean's wish list when he conceived the car, but a fuel-injected 2.8-liter Peugeot-Renault-Volvo V-6 actually occupied the midships engine bay. Making 130 bhp and 162 pound-feet of torque, it could propel the DMC-12 to 60 mph in 10 to 10.5 seconds—not up to predictions. A five-speed manual transmission was standard with a three-speed automatic optional. Goodyear NCT radial tires that were wider in back than in front were used in an effort to counteract oversteer from the tail-heavy design.

In the long production delay, the starting price more than doubled to $25,000, and sales in the U.S. started just before a crippling recession set in. The company was strapped for cash anyway—a pricey Manhattan headquarters and DeLorean's personal taste for costly air travel by Concorde didn't help. In October 1982 DeLorean was charged with conspiracy to obtain and distribute cocaine to raise money for the firm. He was acquitted in 1984, but the factory was closed in December 1982. The last few of the 9080 cars made were sold as '83s.

The DMC-12 could have faded to black. Then Hollywood came calling. Made into a "time machine" for three *Back to the Future* films, the car is now a pop-culture hero.

1981
Ford Thunderbird
Town Landau Coupe

Since the late Fifties, Ford had done an excellent job of cultivating the personal-luxury image of the Thunderbird. By the early Seventies, it practically became a shadow Lincoln Continental Mark IV. Then Dearborn tacked in a different direction, and a car that had been admired jumped to wildly popular overnight.

Every pendulum swing has its counter motion, however. Thunderbird's came with the 1980–82 eighth generation.

The 1977–79 T-Birds were the nameplate's all-time popularity leaders, averaging 318,344 per model year. Part of their allure was a considerable drop in price—the intent being to make them more competitive with the Chevrolet Monte Carlo, sales leader in the "affordable" end of the surging personal-luxury segment. These 'Birds shared a chassis with the midsize LTD II (née Torino).

When Ford's aged intermediates were retired in '79, the next Thunderbird would need to find another host. The unitized "Fox" platform that made its debut with the 1978 Ford Fairmont and Mercury Zephyr compacts (and was enabling the Mustang to fully return to its "ponycar" roots) was picked for the job. It might have been asking too much.

Against the '79, this T-Bird was shorter by 16 inches, narrower by 4.4 inches, and trimmer in wheelbase by 5.6 inches at 108.4. It was lighter by as much as 950 pounds.

Styling crammed 1977–79 cues onto a smaller surface. Front suspension was now by MacPherson struts. Variable-ratio rack-and-pinion steering and power-assisted front disc/rear drum brakes were used. A new 122-bhp 4.2-liter (255-cid) V-8 was standard in base and Town Landau models and a 5.0-liter (302-cube) engine was ensconced in the Silver Anniversary version, but an 88-horse 3.3-liter straight six—a first for a Thunderbird—was added as a late-season delete option. A four-speed overdrive automatic transmission came with the bigger V-8 and the Town Landau and Anniversary got a standard digital instrument cluster.

However, at 156,803 orders, T-Bird demand drooped by almost 45 percent. As bad as that was, it would look healthy compared to 86,693 in 1981 and 45,142 in '82.

For 1981, the six became standard in the base and Town Landau cars, and the 4.2 settled into the Heritage, the new name for the Silver Anniversary. Halogen headlamps were standardized and front head and legroom were increased. In '82 a 3.8-liter V-6 powered the Heritage, but most had the 4.2 V-8—the 302 was dropped entirely.

The pendulum would swing again. A new sleek, aerodynamic '83 began a generation that invigorated T-Bird sales.

1985
Ford Mustang SVO
Hatchback Coupe

I n late September 1980, the Ford Mustang was ending the second year of a return to its genuine "ponycar" nature after the 1974–78 run of the Mustang II that used subcompact Pinto underpinnings. At the same time, Ford Motor Company President Donald Petersen announced a new department that would, among other things, develop special production models with racing-derived technology. The group was called Special Vehicle Operations (SVO). Its first project would be a Mustang quite unlike any before.

That car, the Mustang SVO, arrived with the 1984 model year. Its key feature was a turbocharged and intercooled four-cylinder engine, but it offered a lot more.

Though the Mustangs built since '79 sprang from the cor-

porate "Fox" platform with MacPherson-strut front suspension and four-link/coil-spring rear suspension, a vestige of the Pinto days remained in the form of a standard 2.3-liter (140-cid) ohc four-cylinder engine. There were even turbocharged versions of this engine in 1979–80 and 1983–84, but they did not have the SVO's air-to-air intercooler (a first on an American car), "torque control" that amped up turbo boost to a maximum 14 pounds per square inch gauge pressure, or electronic engine-management controls. As introduced, the port-fuel-injected powerplant made 174 bhp at 4400 rpm and 210 pound-feet of torque at 3000 rpm.

The '84 Mustang SVO cost a whopping $15,596, a lot by Mustang standards of the day. Buyers got a five-speed

manual transmission with overdrive, a limited-slip rear axle with 3.45:1 gears, Koni adjustable shock absorbers, and a couple of things the engineering team pushed for—four-wheel ventilated disc brakes and 16×7-inch cast-alloy five-lug wheels. Ford claimed a 7.7-second time for a 0–60-mph run and 15.8 seconds in the quarter mile.

Appearance specifics started with a blunt, essentially grilleless front for improved aerodynamics and a hood with a scoop that funneled air directly to the intercooler to aid in its mission to cool the charge to the cylinders and hike horsepower. Large, recessed twin headlights replaced the quad lamps on other Mustangs. A standard bilevel polycarbonate rear spoiler added downforce.

The car's goals were to explore ways to get V-8-like performance from a smaller,

more fuel-efficient engine and compete against sophisticated European machinery in on-road dynamics. *Road & Track* felt it "may be the best all-around car for the enthusiast driver ever produced by the U.S. industry."

However, it was a package somewhat alien to traditional Mustang fanciers and not enough to lure import intenders. Just 4508 were produced that first year.

The '85s started out with a price cut of more than $1000, a racier 3.73:1 axle, and a change to constant-ratio steering. Late in the model year came engine modifications that pushed horsepower to 200 and torque to 240 pound-feet. These cars got new flush-face headlights, too. Still, production dropped to 1954 units. Almost unchanged, SVO gave it one more go in '86, when a final 3382 were made.

1985
Cadillac
Eldorado Coupe

The 1985 model year marked the end of an incredibly successful period in the history of the Cadillac Eldorado as a front-wheel-drive personal-luxury car. Made in five series from 1967 to 2002, it was the third-generation 1979–85 Eldos that individually ranked as the seven best production years ever posted by the E-body Cadillac. Model-year production never fell below 52,685, and from 1980 to '85 the Eldorado handily outsold its leading domestic rivals, the Lincoln Mark VI and Mark VII.

The gen-three Eldo figured in the third phase of General Motors's late-Seventies downsizing campaign. Engineered in unison with the Oldsmobile Toronado and Buick Riviera, the personal coupes were styled with references to their respective predecessors. Despite being considerably smaller—the Eldorado shed 20 inches of bumper-to-bumper length, 8.4 inches of width, and 12.3 inches of wheelbase—the trio still imparted a sense of luxury and authority. On all, a nearly vertical backlight brought a formal look to the roofline, helping to visually extend rear deck length while actually maximizing rear-seat headroom. Flush mounting of the deeply sloped windshield reduced wind noise.

A Biarritz option package allowed Eldo owners to gild the lily and Touring Coupe equipment available from 1982 on

featured European-style handling and appearance touches. In 1984–85 there was convertible, the first since 1976.

Eldorado—and the other Es—utilized four-wheel independent suspension, a first for front-drive cars. The personal Caddy used various engines between '79 and '85—not all to great effect. The 350-cid gasoline V-8 of 1979 (and '80 in California) performed well, as did a 49-state 368 V-8 in 1980. But a 368 converted to electronic cylinder deactivation in '81 was rough in its "V8-6-4" transitions. A base 249-cid "HT 4100" new in '82 was trouble prone. So was a 350 diesel. A V-6 option was offered for just two years.

A new, smaller Eldorado in the works for 1985 was delayed by a year, and fortunately so, it turned out. Thus, the '79-generation car got one more turn. A base coupe—sans Biarritz or Touring Coupe package—like the car shown started at $20,931. The 76,401 Eldos built (including 2300 convertibles) ranked as the second most ever made for a year, topped only by the 77,806 from 1984.

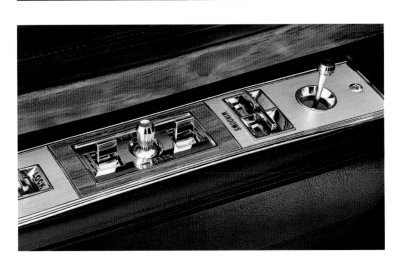

1985
Chevrolet Camaro
Z28 IROC-Z Coupe

"Racing improves the breed" has been one of the automotive world's core beliefs for a long, long time. Racing—or at least the promotion of it—certainly improved the Chevrolet Camaro Z28 in 1985.

The International Race of Champions (IROC) was an exhibition racing series that pitted top drivers from varied disciplines in matched cars. It crowned champions annually from 1974 to 1980, then resumed in 1984. Starting in '75, the series' celebrated drivers strapped into race-prepped Camaros. Chevrolet eventually took advantage of this connection by putting the IROC label on street cars.

IROC-Zs were made from 1985 to 1990. Through '87, the IROC was an option package for the most muscular Camaro, the Z28. In the final three years of the run, it fully replaced the Z28 as the highest-performance version of Chevy's "ponycar."

At its introduction, the IROC-Z package added $695 to the cost of a Z28 coupe. It included grille-mounted fog lights, body-color rocker trim, "ground-effects" aero bits that wrapped the car's lower edges, and large "IROC-Z" decals on the doors. Chassis changes included upgrades to the front struts, springs, and jounce bumpers that low-

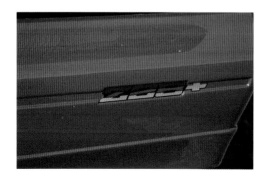

ered ride height by 15mm compared to the Z28; Delco/ Bilstein gas rear shock absorbers; a larger-diameter rear stabilizer; and a tubular cross brace to reinforce the front frame rails. Valving of the steering gear was revised for higher effort and additional road feel. Rolling stock was 245/50VR16 Goodyear Eagle GT "Gatorback" unidirectional-tread tires on specific 16×8 aluminum wheels. Color selections were limited to White, Silver, Black, Yellow, Bright Blue Metallic, and Red.

Buyers could choose one of three 5.0-liter (305-cid) "small-block" V-8s, starting with a 155-bhp job joined to a five-speed manual or extra-cost four-speed automatic transmission. With a freer-flowing exhaust (but only with the stickshift), 190 horsepower was on tap—and was exclusive to the IROC-Z.

Those engines had four-barrel carburetors, but tuned-port fuel injection fed the final engine choice, which pumped out 215 bhp at 4400 rpm and 275 pound-feet of torque at 3200 revs. It worked through the automatic trans. With this powerteam, *Motor Trend* was able to reach 60 mph from a standstill in 6.87 seconds and blitz the quarter mile in 15.3 seconds. *MT* writer Ron Grable, an accomplished racer himself, felt the IROC-Z could "humble many Euro/ Japanese cars sporting much fancier window stickers."

The '85 was in the Camaro's third generation that bowed for 1982. Its wedgy F-body outline came from an advanced styling studio headed by General Motors veteran William Porter; Jerry Palmer's Chevy studio completed the look.

A November '84 on-sale date for Camaros that was later than for other 1985 Chevys helped to reduce orders for the Z28 to 68,403 cars for the model year. However, nearly a third of them—21,177—came as IROC-Zs.

1986
Shelby GLH-S Four-Door Hatchback Sedan

Forget a wolf in sheep's clothing. The Shelby GLH-S wanted to be Godzilla in sheep's clothing. It funneled loads of horsepower through the front wheels of an otherwise-sensible subcompact hatchback platform that began life as a humble Dodge Omni.

The GLH-S was another of former sports car racer Carroll Shelby's self-branded transformations of an existing production car. As he had done with Ford Mustangs 20 years earlier, Shelby took some 1986 Omnis under his wing at the Shelby American works in Whittier, California. The result was one of the quickest cars of the time, appearances notwithstanding.

Omni and its Plymouth sibling, the Horizon, were new for 1978. They not only solidly got Chrysler into the subcompact field that arose in the Seventies (it had been modestly coping via Hillman and Mitsubishi captive imports), but they foretold a sea change in American car design. They were the first domestically produced cars with transverse engines and front-wheel drive similar to "world cars" (like the Volkswagen Golf/Rabbit) that were coming to the fore.

Indeed, the "Omnirizon"—as the near-twins were sometimes called—came out of a project begun by Chrysler Europe. That explains the boxy four-door hatchback body with minimal front and rear overhangs on a 99.1-inch wheelbase—though 2+2 fastback coupes with some of the same engineering did join the fold in 1979.

The emphases of these cars were, of course, fuel economy, affordability, and utility. That didn't leave much room for fun, but Chrysler Corporation had a new man at the helm, Lee Iacocca, and he wanted to have a few laughs.

As in his former Ford days, Iacocca got in touch with Shelby to provide to some of his proven performance magic. The Chrysler Shelby Performance Center was set up near Los Angeles for this purpose. One of the products of the effort was the 1984 Omni GLH—Shelby said it stood for "Goes Like Hell"—with 110 bhp from a massaged version of the Chrysler-built 2.2-liter ohc "Trans-4" engine that had been around since 1981. The next year saw the arrival of a turbocharged 2.2, a GLH option that raised horsepower to 146—and worsened the prodigious torque-steer of the "rabbit-eater," as Shelby termed this faster, lower-cost rival to VW's "hot hatch" GTI.

Some guys just can't have enough fun it seems. Shelby took one last crack at making the Omni more of a mini monster, but this he did under his own roof. He called it the GLH-S: "Goes Like Hell-S'more."

Under the hood was the first sighting of the Turbo II version of the 2.2 powerplant, augmented with multiport fuel injection, a larger turbocharger—with intercooler—and an improved intake. These changes spurred output to 175 bhp. As with the Dodge GLH, a five-speed manual was the required gearbox. Standstill-to-60-mph sprints dropped to a reported 6.5 seconds, a good second faster than with the 146-horse engine. Upgrades to the suspension and fat Goodyear Gatorback rubber improved handling.

Save for graphics and wheels, the Shelby GLH-S looked like a Dodge Omni GLH, but it wasn't priced like one. The 500 made stickered at $10,995, a $3077 upcharge.

P ontiac made a big push in the 1986 NASCAR season. Bill Elliot in his Ford Thunderbird had been killing Pontiac and the other General Motors cars on the superspeedways, where speeds exceeded 200 mph (though Darrell Waltrip piloted a Chevrolet Monte Carlo as he scored the most points in the '85 season). The superior aerodynamics of the T-Bird meant that it could not only go faster, but its rear end stayed planted when coming out of corners at high speeds.

To win, Pontiac needed a better shape for the Grand Prix that its teams were using. A new droop snoot was far slipperier than the upright Grand Prix grille. However, more effort was expended on altering the tail.

The GP's formal notchback roofline added to rear-end instability. To counter that, a large "bubbleback" rear window and a rear spoiler were added to smooth airflow and cut rear-end lift. Pontiac developed the rear window in a wind tunnel on a race-car and then adapted the window to fit a car for the street. As

Pontiac was working over the GP, Chevrolet was doing similar things to the related Monte Carlo SS, except Chevy designed its sloping rear window for the street car first and then adapted it for racing.

To homologate the modifications for acceptance by NASCAR, Pontiac had to sell an aerodynamic version of its rear-wheel-drive Grand Prix personal-luxury coupe to the public. The division called it the 2+2, a label cribbed from a hot Pontiac of the Sixties. The elongated, fixed rear window left an opening under the short fiberglass trunklid just wide enough to extract the compact spare tire. Rear seats did not fold down, and a long parcel shelf sealed off the top of the trunk area. A single color scheme was offered.

The 2+2 was fortified with a sport suspension and limited-slip differential. It was powered by a 165-bhp 305-cid V-8 with four-barrel carburetion. (The Chevrolet Monte Carlo SS had an 180-bhp version of that engine.)

Performance was brisk for the era, but perhaps not as fast as the aero look suggested. *Car and Driver* coaxed a 2+2 through the 0–60-mph sprint in 10.2 seconds and ran the quarter mile in 17.6 seconds at 80 mph.

Base prices of notchback GPs ran from $10,259 to $11,579, but the 2+2 started at a hefty $18,214. Only 1225 were built for '86, its sole year on the market.

Meanwhile, back at the speedways, both Pontiac and its most-celebrated driver, Richard Petty, expected great things of the 2+2. But no good deed seemingly goes unpunished. As Greg Fielden explained in the book *NASCAR Chronicle*, "[I]nstead of cutting the air smoothly, the car turned out to be an ill-handling beast. Petty failed to win a race." In the '86 season's final points count, Chevy chauffeurs Dale Earnhardt, Waltrip, and Tim Richmond placed one, two, and three, respectively. Elliott and Ricky Rudd followed in Fords. Rusty Wallace was the top Poncho pilot in sixth place.

1987
Buick Regal
GNX Coupe

fter 10 model years, the turbocharged Buick V-6 had come to this: an advertised 276 bhp at 4400 rpm and 360 pound-feet of torque at 3000 rpm, enough to hurl a 3500-plus-pound five-passenger midsize coupe to 60 mph in 4.7 seconds, through the quarter-mile traps at less than 14 seconds, and on to a computer-limited 124-mph top speed. A stock Chevrolet Corvette of the day, "America's sports car," couldn't accelerate as fast.

The Buick that could do all those things was the black-as-night 1987 Regal GNX. It was a rare and glorious send-off for the generation of rear-wheel-drive, body-on-frame, G-body cars about to give way to a wholly redesigned and engi-neered family of intermediates. It was collectible practically from the day it appeared and has been ever since.

That the GNX could outrun a Corvette in a straight line was no accident of birth. The engineers behind it planned

things that way. After wrangling with division management for approval—the brand was then transitioning to a "mature" and "substantial" marketing image—and calling on outside help from ASC/McLaren for engine and chassis enhancements, they got the car they wanted.

There was a template for the GNX, the Regal Grand National. Introduced in 1982 to let Buick brag about its NASCAR manufacturer's championship from the previous season, it took a year off before coming back in '84 with a better 200-bhp turbo V-6 and mean noir looks. Two years later, the engine got sequential fuel injection and an intercooler to jump to 235 (later 245) horsepower.

Off this background the Buick personnel went to work on the GNX. On McLaren's advice, they used a lighter, faster-responding ceramic turbine. Freer-flowing heads and low-restriction dual exhaust also boosted power. ASC tackled stiffening the body and making rear-suspension changes to improve stability. Special lace-type 16-inch wheels and wide tires fit under broad composite fender flares.

The extra care resulted in a car that cost $29,290—$14,154 more than a Grand National. Just 547 were made.

1988
Lincoln Mark VII LSC Coupe

Given that Lincoln labeled its personal-luxury hardtop released in April 1968 the Continental Mark III, it was clear that it regarded the car to be in the bloodline of the original Continental of 1940–48 and ultra-expensive Continental Mark II of 1956–57. The second restart would touch off an unbroken string of Mark-series Lincolns destined to run for 30 years, ending with the last Mark VIII.

Classical lines draped these cars through the downsized Mark VI of 1980–83, but its significantly reduced sales convinced management a new direction was needed. Along with daring styling, the 1984–92 Mark VII sought to give drivers a more sporting experience via a model called LSC.

The rounder, smoother Mark VII shed many of the appearance hallmarks of earlier Marks but did keep a formal chrome grille and hint of a spare-tire cover in the trunklid. The windshield was canted at a wind-cheating 60-degree slope. All of this wrapped a car built from the corporate "Fox" unit-body platform.

There were base and familiar "designer" décor models, but the intriguing newcomer was the LSC, the so-called hot rod Lincoln. It had a more purposeful look with a black, ribbed lower-body molding and distinct aluminum wheels with 215/65R15 blackwall tires. Inside was a leather-wrapped steering wheel and gearshift knob. A more aggressive 3.27:1 final drive made for hastier getaways (but the 140-bhp 5.0-liter V-8 was shared with other Mark VIIs). Air springs were firmer, antiroll bars were thicker, and steering was quicker.

The LSC was improved in the next two years. Four-wheel antilock brakes and a 180-horse engine became standard in '85. Analog gauges and 200 bhp—thanks to sequential multipoint fuel injection—arrived for 1986.

The next big change hit for the 1988 model, which bowed in March '87. (The long run led to 38,259 assemblies, the VII's best model-year total.) Remaining models—Bill Blass and LSC, both starting at $25,016—got a fresh wavy-surface grille and a 225-bhp "H.O." V-8 from the Ford Mustang GT that really stepped up performance. The LSC adopted 16-inch wheels in a new turbine-vane design.

1989
Pontiac Firebird
Trans Am GTA Coupe

W hat do you do when the "most" Pontiac Firebird, the Trans Am, is not enough? You make it a Trans Am GTA. That is what Pontiac did in 1987 to stir the souls of T/A shoppers, and it was a ploy that worked well for a while.

In its first year, the GTA made up 33.8 percent of the Trans Ams made. However, from 1988 to 1990 it was the choice of a majority of Trans Am customers. In 1989, the year from when the car shown hails, 9631 GTAs outsold the standard T/A by 3904 units, even though the GTA starting price poked through the $20,000 barrier for the first time.

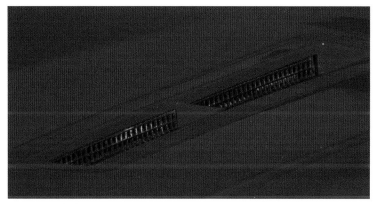

The '89s were part of the Firebird's third generation, which by then was on its downside. Fresh for 1982, the design was destined to be replaced in 1993. An F-body cousin to the Chevrolet Camaro, it sprang from the same central advanced-styling concept, which was subject to much wind-tunnel testing. It became defined as a Firebird in John Schinella's Pontiac Studio. For distinction from its Chevy counterpart, third-generation Firebirds would maintain some changing semblance of the brand's spilt-grille look and go their own way with hideaway headlights.

One place in which the two cars were unfailingly linked was in the engine bay. After 1981, Pontiac ceased making its own V-8 engine. From that point it started using the 5.0-liter (305-cid) and 5.7-liter (350-cid) mills from Chevrolet to power V-8-equipped Firebirds.

The specific look of the 1989 Trans Am traced back to '85, when a revised nose with an air dam that incorporated fog lamps and a symmetrical hood with twin groups of louvers came into use. A new wraparound style of rear spoiler was a 1986 addition. The stage was now set for the GTA.

As performance cars continued to make a comeback in the Eighties, the horsepower race was heating up again. Pontiac added the 5.7-liter V-8—basically a Corvette engine with a more restrictive intake—to the mix for 1987. At 210 bhp it ceded 15 horsepower to that year's Ford Mustang 5.0-liter engine, but it developed more torque. The 5.7,

available only with an automatic transmission, was a core element of the GTA. To go with the engine Pontiac threw in the WS6 sport suspension (with four-wheel disc brakes), 16-inch gold-toned "diamond-spoke" alloy wheels, articulated seats with inflatable lumbar supports, body-color lower exterior cladding, and specific badging throughout. Pontiac said a GTA was capable of a 14.5-second quarter-mile run and 60 mph in 6.5 seconds.

In 1988, the tuned-port-injection 5.7 grew to 225 bhp and the GTA picked up standard power accessories, air conditioning, and stereo controls built into the steering wheel. Another 10 horsepower arrived for 1989.

The 1989 GTA was the basis for a highly interesting—and quite collectible—special, the Indianapolis 500 Pace Car 20th Anniversary Trans Am. As the name implies, the GTA was selected to pace the 500-mile classic that year, but instead of a Chevy "small-block," it was powered by the turbocharged V-6 from the late lamented Buick Regal GNX, modified to generate an advertised 250 bhp. Along with that, the anniversary cars got bigger front brake rotors, a white paint job, light-tan interior, special identification, and a replica set of pace-car door graphics that could be applied at the buyer's discretion. A T-top roof was optional for any of the 1555 that were built.